EVANGELISM FOR OUR GENERATION

Jim Petersen

NAVPRESS

A MINISTRY OF THE NAVIGATORS

P.O. Box 6000, Colorado Springs, Colorado 80934

The Navigators is an international Christian organization. Jesus Christ gave His followers the Great Commission to go and make disciples (Matthew 28:19). The aim of The Navigators is to help fulfill that commission by multiplying laborers for Christ in every nation.

NavPress is the publishing ministry of The Navigators. NavPress publications are tools to help Christians grow. Although publications alone cannot make disciples or change lives, they can help believers learn biblical discipleship, and apply what they learn to their lives and ministries.

© 1985 by Jim Petersen
All rights reserved, including translation
Library of Congress Catalog Card
    Number: 84-63114
ISBN: 0-89109-476-8
14761

Second printing, 1985

All Scripture quotations are from *The Holy Bible: New International Version* (NIV). Copyright © 1973, 1978, 1984, International Bible Society. Used by permission of Zondervan Bible Publishers.

Printed in the United States of America

Contents

To Marge and our children,
who have illuminated The Way
for many by the light
of their lives.

Preface

This book is a sequel to *Evangelism as a Lifestyle*. It is motivated to a great extent by the reader response to the first book. Many committed readers have provided information, expressed appreciation, and, most importantly, asked questions. This positive feedback has indicated that the first book struck a responsive chord and that the subject of evangelism as a lifestyle is pertinent and timely. The probing questions from readers have led to my realization that a second book would be helpful and that many people are looking for guidance on how to proceed.

In *Evangelism as a Lifestyle* I focused attention on the fact that we Christians are reaching very little of our world with the message of Christ. This fact is obvious on the global level when we simply catalogue the world's population. That it is true regarding our own society is evident from the deterioration of values and from the major segments of our society that are totally unreached and unaffected by Christian values. We also experience this need for a new approach to evangelism on the individual level among our friends, relatives, and associates.

The world around us on all levels is becoming increasingly secularized and less receptive to approaches that were effective in the past. As Christians we are surrounded by this nonChristian society, but we almost seem to be unaware of its existence. Our evangelism is primarily among the strays from our own fold, people who have grown up in our churches. Caring for this fruit, together with attending to the internal needs of our churches, is enough to keep us busy. Consequently, there is little occasion to pause to reflect on the fact that we are not doing well at reaching out to the secularized world around us. In a sense, we are talking to ourselves and don't even realize it.

The intent of *Evangelism as a Lifestyle* was to call attention to this situation, and to suggest a solution. The book is basically a Bible study on the biblical patterns of evangelism. I emphasized that evangelism is a process, consisting of sowing, watering, cultivating, and reaping. Many steps are involved as people travel the long pathway from darkness to light.

Christians have traditionally concentrated on a single phase of the evangelizing process: proclamation. The result is what we have called a "reaping mentality," where evangelism is limited to a quick presentation of the essence of the gospel, anticipating an immediate decision. Of course, proclamation is indeed the thing to do in the right situation. This is what Peter did in Jerusalem on the day of Pentecost when three thousand people responded. This is what Philip did with the Ethiopian and what Paul did in the synagogues everywhere he went.

In *Evangelism as a Lifestyle* I emphasized, through a study of the New Testament, that a religious heritage is a prerequisite to effective *proclamation*. The scope of proclamation is limited to the prepared. A more complete definition of evangelism was outlined by Jesus and expanded in the epistles. We called this *affirmation*—a process of modeling and explaining the Christian message.

Upon reflection, it seems that it was not completely accurate to refer to two modes of evangelism: proclamation and affirmation. It would be more accurate to say that proclamation is a form of reaping, the final step in the process of evangelism.

Affirmation of the gospel involves three simultaneous witnesses: the witness of our lives, the witness of the body, and the verbal witness. Thus it becomes a *process* of modeling and explaining the Christian message.

When we understand evangelism in these terms, it becomes possible for the Christian to enjoy a lifetime of personal involvement and fruitfulness. Because of our various gifts, all of us can participate in the process. The verbal witness, which seems so difficult for many of us, falls into the context of a process where it becomes more natural. This also means we can effectively reach those who are not yet ready to respond to proclamation. Those previously regarded as unreachable become accessible.

Chapter 22 of *Evangelism as a Lifestyle* is entitled "Suggestions for Application." Nearly all the readers' questions and comments related to this chapter, thus underscoring the need for more practical guidance in the process of affirmation evangelism. Part Two of this book is my attempt to answer those questions and to meet this need. Even in this context, however, I want to communicate *principles* that will serve as a basis for action. Please do not interpret these principles as a method or utilize the illustrations as patterns to be repeated. Principles are universal, but methods can apply only in a specific context. Affirmation evangelism involves living in a dynamic relationship, and this cannot be stereotyped. The rigid repetition of methods cannot provide an adequate foundation for the dynamic and flexible relationships involved.

My purpose, then, in Part Two is not to write a "how to" manual but to provide concepts and ideas for your own adaptation.

Before we get to this practical part of the book, we need to take a new look at contemporary man and the direction of his rapidly accelerating change. In addition, we will examine how Jesus related to the people of His times. Together with *Evangelism as a Lifestyle,* this first section will form the basis from which we can proceed to practical applications.

My prayer is that "you may be active in sharing your faith, so that you will have a full understanding of every good thing we have in Christ" (Philemon 6).

PART ONE

The People of Our Generation, and Our Message

Introduction

Ken Lottis has been my colleague in Brazil for twenty years. In recounting the adventures of a recent furlough, he told me the following story.

> As I drove up to the coffee shop that afternoon, I really didn't know what to expect. I hadn't seen Pastor Ellsworth in over twenty years. Now, after all this time, he had tracked me down with a letter and some phone calls. Together with his wife he was driving 165 miles to have a cup of coffee with my wife and me.
>
> When we had first become acquainted, he was newly married, recently ordained, and holding his first pastorate. I

too was recently married at that time, involved in a Navigator ministry and attending his church. Now, twenty years later, we were about to meet in a hotel coffee shop. My wife wondered as we walked in the door, "Do you suppose we will even recognize them?"

We did, probably because they were something of a mirror image of us: a bit of gray hair, a few extra pounds, and some wrinkles around the eyes.

As we began our discussion, we mostly reminisced and talked about our families. Then the conversation shifted to the ministries we had been involved in during those twenty years. Pastor Ellsworth had held several different pastorates, each a bit larger than the previous one. His current church in a midwestern town was typical middle America—farmers, ranchers, etc.

My twenty years had been spent in a Navigator ministry in Brazil. When I mentioned some of our experiences communicating the gospel to young Brazilians, he responded by saying, "In every congregation I have been in I have tried the traditional methods of evangelism: crusades, house-to-house calling, personal evangelism seminars. I picked up *Evangelism as a Lifestyle* because I knew it was about your work with Jim Petersen in Brazil. As I began to read, I suddenly had the feeling that I was finding some explanations for my frustration in my attempts to evangelize the people in our community.

"Our church is a Bible-believing, Bible-preaching church like hundreds of others in the Midwest. The community is small, with a population under ten thousand. Last year I had a week-long series of evangelistic meetings. The evangelist was good and the meetings were well attended, but mostly by people from our own congregation.

"In reading about things you did in Brazil among the secularized, I finally realized that there were many people in my community who were secularized. They were not intellectuals; they were simply people for whom the Church and its message no longer held any interest. They were never going to walk through the doors of my church. I am now asking myself what I have to do to reach them."

This story illustrates one of the primary difficulties we Christians seem to be having in coming to grips with secularization: It is hard to recognize it when we see it.

Although secularism and secularization have joined the list of household words used to describe the prevailing world view of our society, our understanding of these terms is fuzzy. Frequently I get the impression that when people think of a "secularized" person, they get a mental image of someone who is off-beat. Such a strange person can most easily be found in a spiritually-resistant pocket of the country, in a place like San Francisco or New York, and lives some sort of an alternative lifestyle. As one person put it, "I would really like to become involved with secularized people, but I don't think we have any around here."

The secularized people of our society are usually not off-beat at all. They shave. They go to the hairdresser. They wear suits and ties. They car-pool our kids, run our local businesses, and farm our land. We are surrounded by the secularized. Middle America *is* secularized!

There exists an abundance of definitions for secularization. Most of them are essentially in agreement, the central idea being that the secularized person has declared, consciously or perhaps unconsciously, his independence from God. His quasi-religious ideology is based on his faith in science, economics, and technology. He looks to these to answer man's questions and to meet society's needs.

Os Guinness helps clear the fog by making a distinction beween secularism, secularization, and the secularized. *Secu-*

larism is a philosophy. As such it can be analyzed and defined with precision. *Secularization* is a process by which religious ideas become less and "less meaningful and religious institutions more marginal."[1] Secularization rubs off on people. Unlike the philosophy, it is contagious, so that wherever modernization goes, some degree of infection is inevitable. The *secularized* are the people who have been infected. There are different degrees of infection, and Christians are not immune to its influences.[1]

It is probably these degrees of infection that confuse us. We tend to polarize things to extremes in our definitions. We define things in terms of black and white: People are either religious or secularized. As a result, we usually fail to recognize secularization, except when we encounter an individual who is suffering from a terminal infection.

The purpose of this part of the book is to give a greater understanding of the people of our times and a clearer view of what the essence of our message to them should be.

NOTES
1. Os Guinness, *The Gravedigger File* (London: Hodder and Stoughton, 1983), pages 52-53.

1
Understanding the Times

There were once "men of Issachar, who understood the times and knew what Israel should do" (1 Chronicles 12:32).

Sons of Issachar, where are you now?

The Western world is in a cultural shift that offers a bewildering challenge to those who would understand it. To grasp the nature and significance of what has already happened is an elusive task. To read the trends in order to understand where they are taking us is even more difficult.

Futurologists are proliferating the racks with books and periodicals containing a broad range of interpretations and predictions. This makes interesting and enlightening reading. But the changes are coming so fast that often what these writers have to say is dated by the time it reaches the reader. To add to the confusion, there are fundamental differences in their perceptions.

It is not my intention to add one more analysis of our society to those already in existence. Rather, it is to identify, with the broadest of brush strokes, the prevailing trends that characterize our society. My purpose in this chapter is not so much to inform the reader of what is happening as it is to sensitize him to the fact of change—that our society *is* in flux.

Change tends to get past us unnoticed, while we carry on with business as usual. But, for the sake of the Great Commission, we cannot afford to let this happen. We who are Christians are commissioned to work as co-laborers together with God in this world. We must, therefore, seek to understand the times, for the people we are sent to reach are caught up in them. If we fail to understand this basic reality, then we will fail to communicate. We will be talking to people as they once were, before they moved on. We must be alert!

PERCEPTIONS OF THE TRENDS: WHAT ARE THE ANALYSTS SAYING?

Predictions concerning the spiritual climate of our society vary widely. Some foresee a period of unusual receptivity to spiritual values. Others are predicting the opposite.

The optimists. Rifkin and Howard make some very optimistic projections for the growth of the Church. They say, "A growing number of historians, ecologists, economists and anthropologists ask: What will replace materialism? Most agree that . . . the focus of human existence will change from the horizontal plane of materialism to the vertical plane of spiritualism. Only a massive spiritual upheaval, they argue, can provide both the elements of a new world view and the faith and discipline needed to put it into practice."[1] This is indeed a positive note.

In the same vein, John Naisbitt says the United States is undergoing a revival in religious belief and church attendance. This is happening because "during turbulent times many people need structure—not ambiguity—in their lives."[2] People need something to hang on to, to provide an anchor during a transitional age.

George Gallup conducted a religious survey of Americans in 1977. He observed that "the cumulative evidence suggests that the late seventies could, in fact, mark the beginning of a religious revival in America."[3]

These observers of a positive religious trend rely on a common set of indicators to document their analysis. They call attention to the fact that "42 percent of all adults in America attend religious services at least once a week"; that "nearly one in every three Americans now claim to have been 'born again'"; that today "1300 radio stations—one out of every seven in America—is Christian owned and operated"; and that evangelical publishers now account for a third of the total domestic commercial book sales.[4]

It is true! There *is* a boom in evangelical Christianity in America. Anyone can verify this fact by the simple exercise of working his way through the Sunday morning traffic jam surrounding any one of the many super-churches that dot the American scene. The euphoria that seems to characterize these churches, as the overworked pastoral staffs attempt to cope with their own success, gives little occasion to pause and reflect on the bigger picture. Every success indicator confirms that things have never been better.

So Howard and Rifkin conclude, "Of two things we can be sure: a massive religious awakening is in the offing and the first rumblings of this change can already be heard."[5] Are they right?

The pessimists. But there are dissonant evaluations of the religious future of America that are made with equal certainty and with equally impressive documentation. These other voices must sound very strange indeed to Christians who are engrossed in the church growth described above. Kenneth Kantzer, former editor of *Christianity Today,* states, "We may well stand at the end of an era extending from the Reformation to the Russian revolution. A religious ice age is drifting down over Europe and North America (though with significant exceptions in the form of pockets of evangelical vigor). Materialistic paganism has become the dominant world view. This growing secularism, which fashions a culture alien to Christianity, erodes the biblical values in our society and penetrates the church."[6]

What is Kantzer talking about? I believe he is seeing things that have been ignored by the more optimistic observers. He is addressing the bigger picture. The religious trend we just described, impressive as it may be, is not mainstream. It is a countercurrent that is decidedly distinct from the broad flow of the society. In terms of size and impact, the secularized mainstream exerts an overwhelming influence.

Rifkin and Howard recognize the precariousness of the present situation. They observe that "America . . . is made up of two cultures which exist in a carefully structured relationship to one another . . . The Reformation culture of John Calvin [which] remains the basis [and] its bastardized successor, the liberal ethos, superimposed on top."[7] According to them, the question is "whether the new evangelical revival will reshape the American climacteric, or rather be reshaped and absorbed by the secular culture."[8]

Different authors say it in different ways, but most agree that a good part of the world, particularly the Western world, is caught up in this cultural shift. One way of life is dying; it is being replaced by another.

How this shift will affect the spiritual receptivity of the people of our generation is impossible to predict. Much depends on how alert we Christians are to what is happening, and whether or not we will have the flexibility necessary to respond appropriately.

Christopher Lasch identifies the direction he believes society is taking with the title of his book *The Culture of Narcissism*. In it he summarizes the factors that signal the death of what he calls "the culture of competitive individualism," and the emergence of its logical successor, "the pursuit of happiness to the dead end of a narcissistic preoccupation with the self."[9]

Lasch observes that our political theories have lost their capacity to explain events, that our economic theories have suffered the same fate, and that the sciences, once so confident of their ability to provide answers to life, now make it clear that they are not to be looked to for the resolution of the social problems.

The humanities, he says, are as bankrupt as the rest, making the "general admission that humanistic study has nothing to contribute to an understanding of the modern world. Philosophers no longer explain the nature of things or pretend to tell us how to live." The arts claim only to reflect "the artist's inner state of mind." Historians themselves are warning us to beware the "lessons" of history—that they are "not merely irrelevant but dangerous."[10]

Anxiety has added to disillusionment, as society contemplates the consequences of the depletion of our natural resources and the well-founded predictions of ecological disasters. Irrational acts of terrorism and dangerous localized wars make the threat of nuclear annihilation an everyday concern. Inflation renders financial security a tenuous matter. Even the family has lost its earlier function of providing a common life and of child rearing. Social relationships have become tentative and superficial.

Lasch goes on to observe, "As the twentieth century approaches its end, the conviction grows that many other things are ending too. Storm warnings, portents, hints of catastrophe haunt our times. The 'sense of an ending' . . . now pervades the popular imagination."[11]

Since tomorrow is too dubious or too fearsome to contemplate, we absorb ourselves instead in our own private performance. "To live for the moment is the prevailing passion—to live for yourself, not for your predecessors or posterity. . . . Having no hope of improving their lives in any of the ways that matter, people have convinced themselves that what matters is psychic self-improvement: getting in touch with their feelings, eating health food, taking lessons in ballet, immersing themselves in the wisdom of the East, jogging, learning how to 'relate,'" and so on.[12]

And the truth is somewhere in between. The perceptive reader will realize that the optimistic projection of a massive spiritual awakening and the pessimistic prediction of a society imploding into narcissism are both proving to be unrealistic polarizations. Both are overstatements. Both trends continue to be in evidence, but neither gives a balanced picture of what is, in fact, taking place.

In many ways life seems to be strikingly normal. America's youth continue to pursue their traditional goal: success. They are studying; they are concerned about maximizing their potential for success; they are hustling for the financially profitable jobs. There is even a reassuring, though modest, display of concern for politics and social issues.

It almost feels like the "good old days" are back. After the convulsions brought upon us by the generation of the sixties and the indifference and self-gratification that marked the seventies, the scene today seems to be a decided improvement. We finally have a generation that does not seem bent on destroying its own habitat. But this generation is the offspring of the sixties and seventies. Beneath the surface lies the heritage of these two decades. Consequently, the foundations of this generation are more pagan than anything else. The idea of absolute truth is missing. Right and wrong has become something that society decides for itself. And the chief end of all the hard work of society is self-gratification, or hedonism.

There is abundant evidence that these are, in fact, the foundational attitudes of our society. The ease with which we accept abortion; our readiness to divorce and remarry; our indifference toward the psychological health of our children—characteristics such as these are pagan, not Christian! As long as such attitudes prevail, there is little room for debate about the true value system of our society.

This brief vignette of our society should serve to demonstrate the fundamental incompatibility that exists between the belief system of the people who are caught up in the secularized mainstream and the belief system of those of us in the Christian counter-current. While the Christian ethic is rooted in faith, hope, and love, the secular belief system is based on self-centeredness and will result in disillusionment and anxiety.

The people of the secularized mainstream are not really seeking our spiritual values. The idea that the Christian faith could serve as a basis for living never even crosses the minds of most people. Instead, they attempt to satisfy their feelings of inner emptiness and malaise by pursuing experiences that provide momentary illusions of well-being. As one friend of mine put it, "My life consists of going from one experience to another, none of which lasts longer than the time it takes to live it."

GETTING AHEAD OF THE TRENDS

The implications of these trends are multiple and far-reaching, but within the scope of this book one question stands out: What will the effect of all this be on the progress of the gospel in the world?

I believe the answer will be determined by *the manner of our response.* If we continue to carry on and repeat our old success patterns as if the world just described didn't exist, the results will be very easy to predict. But if we respond with understanding and adapt accordingly, we could find the situation serving to the *advantage* of the gospel.

The cultural shift we are discussing is occurring at rapid pace. In *Idols of Destruction,* Herb Schlossberg notes that some "social scientists assign the shift to despair to a single decade: the 1960s."[13] No matter when it first occurred, this negative shift is now readily observable.

I am affiliated with the Christian organization known as The Navigators. Our ministry is primarily to disciple the unreconciled, with the aim of equipping those we win to labor among their peers. This obviously means that we are working in the grass roots, where the early signs of social changes are first perceived.

The trends seem to be running from east to west in the Western world. Europe is being affected first, with the United States following suit. Our European colleagues were among the first to detect the shift to despair.

Changes in approach, content, and expectations were forced on our people in Holland within a short five-year period. In an unpublished paper, Dutch Navigator Gert Doornenbal observes, "The young people of today are not like those we were reaching ten years ago. More and more children are growing up in one-parent homes. Often they lack love and attention."

In Sweden, family counselors talk about "never children." They have never heard anyone say "I love you." They live with unmet emotional needs, wrestling with loneliness and insecurity. They are incapable of normal emotional expression and relationships.[14]

Rinus Baljeu, Dutch Navigator ministering in Sweden, expands on the implication of this situation. He observes, "The 80s started with the shocking discovery that in several countries our evangelism had become a scramble for the very few. We are on our way to becoming a non-religious society. Eighty-five to ninety percent of today's teenagers regard questions like 'Did Jesus live?' or 'Was he the Son of God?' as irrelevant and unimportant."[15]

A British Navigator colleague, John Mulholland, did a limited survey in an effort to understand the extent of secularization among students in England. He said, "The results came as something of a surprise. Students are more secularized than we thought. We have to decide where we should labor: among the relatively few prepared people close to the kingdom of God or among the more secularized. Obviously, the prepared should be reaped, but others are active in reaping this small harvest. Given that those on the secular half of the scale outnumber those on the more biblical half by five to one, the majority of people are substantially secularized. If we are to equip our laborers to work relevantly in the harvest, it is imperative that we learn to work effectively among the secularized and train others to do the same."[16] Every fall this same scramble for "the small harvest among the prepared" is repeated by Christian student organizations on campuses across the United States.

Secularization has reduced the effectiveness of many churches and Christian groups in reaching the world around them. Many spiritual leaders have become greatly discouraged because they feel they are struggling against an overpowering tide. As they become exhausted, motivation drops and doubts about their calling or their doctrine often develop. They begin to feel irrelevant. The simple thing for them to do is to turn their backs on this baffling world and then engross themselves in the familiar, comfortable Christian environment.

Long-established institutions especially suffer these stresses. That which seemed so effective, relevant, and successful a few years ago is not effective today. This kind of declining effectiveness is threatening to any organization. It is also a clear-cut sign that something must be done.

Baljeu observes, "For most countries in Europe today the adaptations we face are not just minor modifications. A major re-evaluation of our whole style and structure is needed. Our patterns of fellowship, our special emphasis and terminology, our organizations, our views on discipleship and standards of conduct—all these need to be reworked so that our ministry, in fact, deals with the needs of those we seek to reach. . . . This is not a matter of becoming more effective. It is a matter of our survival in the 1980s."[17] Anyone who gets a close look at the problems from the vantage of a Christian organization can recognize the urgency and the gravity of the situation.

So the effects of secularization are already upon us. We are not forecasting; we are simply addressing influences that today are powerfully affecting the Church and its mission in the world. The secularized mainstream is rapidly moving away from the values on which the Christian Church rests. But that is no reason for us to give up or to entertain the idea of abandoning certain segments of the population. *Our response should be to work toward understanding the trends and to seek to make them work in favor of the growth of the gospel.* We have a long way to go before that happens. Most of us do not know how to proceed to influence our unchurched contemporaries for Christ.

A VERY TYPICAL STORY

The contrast between the secular world and the Christian subculture is becoming progressively apparent and uncomfortable to many people. A friend of mine described this dilemma in personal terms:

> I was working for a bank in Houston, Texas. I was also a member of a local Baptist church, where I was integrated into a singles group; there were six of us in the group. So my life was made up of two different contexts: my friends from the church and my friends from the bank. Most of my friends at work had a church background, which they had rejected and forsaken. Some didn't have that much. I had a strong desire to bring them to Christ, but every effort resulted in frustration.
>
> Our working relationship was good, and I tried to develop social relationships too. I would attend the bank parties and participate in as many social activities as possible, but there were deep differences between us. In fact, we had so little in common that there was no real communication.
>
> Since I was a relative newcomer in town, some of these friends took the initiative on several occasions to include me in their activities. Once they took me with them to watch the Houston Oilers. But I did not feel comfortable with them. They, of course, sensed this, and it wasn't long before their invitations ceased. My world was the Christian subculture. When I'd leave it, I'd feel insecure and it was easier to go back to my friends from the church.
>
> So that is just what I did. I involved myself in a couple of activities in order to satisfy my desire to be involved in evangelism. For a while I teamed up with a group that visited the local campus to witness to whomever we encountered. Then I participated in the "Here's Life" campaign, evangelizing by

telephone. Both efforts produced some response, but the experiences were inconsequential for my own spiritual development. They did nothing to enrich my own walk with God, because they did not result in an enduring involvement with people who were my peers.

Today as I look back on this experience, I recognize the distance that existed between myself and my friends at the bank. When I was in the middle of it, I couldn't see it. Although they were my peers both socially and intellectually, there was not enough rapport between us for me to be able to sit down and share the gospel openly with them.

This story is so typical. It could certainly be multiplied thousands of times. Fundamental differences that we don't really understand make us fearful and insecure around the unchurched. Because we feel such a distance between "us and them," we carry on as if such people didn't exist. Efforts at evangelism are often either an unannounced assault on a stranger, or little more than being nice to someone.

WHERE IS OUR OFFENSE?

Christian leaders and writers are addressing the fact of secularization. Indeed, it is difficult to pick up a Christian magazine that does not contain some reference to secularization and its effects. The problem is that, almost without exception, the objective of such articles is to make us aware of threats against our religious liberties and human rights.

Thus "humanism" is becoming a household word among Christians. It is understood as being the foremost philosophical alternative to Christianity, the great contemporary enemy. As secularization moves our society away from theistic religion, humanism—faith in man himself—rushes in to fill the vacuum, undermining Christian ethics and values. I would agree that the threat is real.

Although we are indebted to those who are alerting us to the encroachments of secularization and its consequences, it seems to me that something is missing in much of what is being said. We are skilled at spelling out the distance between the positions. We are clear in our warnings and counsel related to endangered rights and freedoms on private and political levels. In short, we are building a great defense. But *where is our offense?*

We are not dealing merely with ideas and philosophies; we are dealing with *people.* Ideas find their existence only in people's minds. In the zeal of our battle against ideas, we Christians often confuse matters by placing ourselves in a position of war against those who hold to those ideas. But we must always remember that we are sent to such people.

A similar situation apparently existed in the first century between the Christians and the Jews. Michael Green points out that Christianity was not distinct from Jewish culture for at least a couple of decades after Jesus' resurrection. Jewish Christians had no thought of separating themselves from the rest of Israel. The Messiah had come! They hoped Israel would come to share this conviction about Jesus. Although the seeds of division were there from the beginning, the Christians of the first century still held on to the hope of winning Israel.

Green observes, "Though violent at times, the Christian approach was inflamed by love . . . and longing to see [Israel] acknowledging their Messiah. But successive turning points . . . changed [this attitude] to one of hatred and antipathy. It was no longer evangelism among the Jews but apologetic against the Jews which interested Christians."[18]

We Christians are running the risk of falling short of the grace of God in the same way today. This book is written with the prayer that we will look upon the people of our time as

Christ does—with compassion on those who are "harassed and helpless, like sheep without a shepherd" (Matthew 9:36). Although it may be necessary to understand the distances between the secular and the Christian positions, our main concern is with building bridges.

NOTES

1. Jeremy Rifkin with Ted Howard, *The Emerging Order* (New York: G.P. Putnam's Sons, 1979), page 95.
2. John Naisbitt, *Megatrends* (New York: Warner Books, 1982), page 240.
3. Rifkin, page 99.
4. Rifkin, pages 99, 101, 105, 112.
5. Rifkin, page 96.
6. Kenneth Kantzer, "Evangelicalism: Mid-course Self-Appraisal," *Christianity Today* (January 7, 1983), page 11.
7. Rifkin, page 129.
8. Rifkin, page 126.
9. Christopher Lasch, *The Culture of Narcissism* (New York: W.W. Norton & Co., Inc., 1979), page xxv.
10. Lasch, page xxiv.
11. Lasch, page 3.
12. Lasch, pages 5, 4.
13. Herbert Schlossberg, *Idols for Destruction* (Nashville: Thomas Nelson Publishers, 1983), page 3.
14. Gert Doornenbal, "Knowing the People of Our Time," (January 1982), page 2.
15. Rinus Baljeu, "Evangelism: Secularization and The Navigators," (August 1982), page 1.
16. John Mulholland and Gary Pryke, "Secularization and Student Evangelism," Reading, Great Britain (September 1983), page 9.
17. Baljeu, page 3.
18. Michael Green, *Evangelism in the Early Church* (Grand Rapids: Eerdmans, 1970), page 105.

2
Understanding the People of Our Generation

Whenever a cultural shift takes place, we know that on the practical level people are changing. For Christians who make up the countercurrent and are not caught up in the change, this can be unsettling. We find ourselves surrounded by people we really do not understand. Our most common response is to ignore or deny the reality of these cultural differences. "After all," we reason, "people are people, and the gospel is the gospel." But effective communication presupposes an understanding between communicator and receiver. And when we make little effort to truly understand, we lose communication.

What are the secular people of our generation really

like? What makes them different from the people of previous generations? In what ways are they different from their Christian contemporaries? How are they similar?

There are three primary factors in man's make-up that determine the answers to these questions. Two of them are constant; they have not altered since the beginning of human history. The third differentiates the people of one generation or culture from another. In one sense it is correct to say that "man is man" the world over. There is a sameness about man wherever and under whatever circumstances he is found. But those who call our attention to the differences between generations and peoples are closer to the whole truth. There are profound differences that categorically separate one people from another.

We need to understand these three characteristics in their proper relationship if we are to communicate effectively beyond the perimeters of our own sub-groups. The three primary factors are:

1. Man is created in God's image.
2. Man is fallen.
3. Man is influenced by his society.

MAN IS CREATED IN GOD'S IMAGE.

Then God said, "Let us make man in our image, in our likeness." . . . So God created man in his own image, in the image of God he created him; male and female he created them. (Genesis 1:26-27)

When God created man, he made him in the likeness of God. He created them male and female; at the time they were created, he blessed them and called them "man." . . . Adam . . . had a son in his own likeness, in his own image; and he named him Seth. (Genesis 5:1-3)

"In [God] we live and move and have our being." As
some of your own poets have said, "We are his offspring."
    Therefore since we are God's offspring, we should not
think that the divine being is like . . . an image made by
man's design and skill. (Acts 17:28-29)

These are the three principle passages in the Bible
about man being made *in God's image.* What does this being in
His image really mean? Perhaps someone somewhere is
satisfied that he has plumbed the depths of this concept, but I
feel that I am still on the surface of it.

We can make a few fragmentary observations based on
the above and related passages: Man is unique and significant. He bears certain resemblances to the God who created
him.

Then we can go on to speculate on the specifics of those
resemblances: God is a person, possessing the ability to plan,
decide, and act. He has personality, with specific attitudes like
love and hate. He communicates, and He exercises creativity
and headship.

Being created in the image of God differentiates man
from the rest of creation. It makes him conscious of his own
uniqueness. Man understands that God has made him different from the rest of the universe. He can relate to God in a
way no other part of creation can. Since God is personal, and
since man is in His image, the nature of this relationship is
also personal. But I suspect the significance of this truth goes
much deeper.

In his last major work before his death, historian Arnold
Toynbee made some observations about man's uniqueness
that help broaden the horizons of our considerations. His
observations are especially interesting because they were
made from an avowed nonChristian position. He prefaced
his comments with the statement, "It is now hardly possible

any longer to believe that the phenomena of which a human being is conscious have been called into existence by the fiat of a human-like creator god."[1]

With this statement Toynbee dismissed Christianity as an invalid source of insight. Consequently, he arrived at his conclusions by observing and contemplating man and life, without reference to God or God's revelation. Then he continued, "But, so far, this no longer tenable traditional hypothesis [of a creator god] has not been replaced by any convincing alternative. . . . The increase in our knowledge . . . has not brought with it an understanding of the nature or the purpose (if there is a purpose) of life and consciousness themselves."[2]

As Toynbee discarded the idea of a Creator God and also the Darwinian thesis, he spelled out the dimensions of the human dilemma: "Every live human being . . . is a conscious purposeful spirit that is physically alive in a material body. None of these components [a conscious spirit and a material body] have ever been encountered apart from the rest. They are always found in association with each other; yet their relation to each other is incomprehensible."[3]

Then Toynbee wondered at the "possession of consciousness and . . . the ability to make plans," and at the ability of human beings to deliberately choose. He asked, "What is the source of these ethical judgements, which apparently are intrinsic to human nature but are foreign to the nature of non-human species? . . . What is the situation and the significance in the Universe of a conscious, purposeful human being, imbued with this sense of the distinction between right and wrong and impelled . . . to do what seems to him to be right? A human being feels as if he is the centre of the Universe because his own consciousness is, for him, the point from which he views the . . . panorama. . . . [Yet] his conscience . . . tells him that, in so far as he gives way to his self-centeredness, he is putting himself morally, as well as intellectually, in the wrong."[4]

Probably all of these very perceptive observations on the uniqueness of man-nature find their explanation in these three words: "in God's image." For, whatever else it means, it at least tells us that man is inescapably self-conscious and inescapably God-conscious. There is something there within man that keeps him struggling with the riddle of his own consciousness—until he acknowledges God.

Recently I led an evangelistic open-Bible study with some university students. When it came time for questions, one student, in all seriousness, asked, "Could someone explain to me why I am here in this room? I have never been interested in these things, yet here I am. What is it that compels me to search? Why can't I be content to live without questioning?"

Man is created in God's image; therefore, he has a natural receptivity to spiritual truth. All evangelism is predicated on this fact.

MAN IS FALLEN.

Three calamities overtook man when he fell: (1) he came to know good and evil; (2) his life became futile; and (3) he died. It is hard to tell which calamity is the most painful to live with.

Man knows good and evil. The serpent said to Eve, "God knows that when you eat of [the tree] your eyes will be opened, and you will be like God, knowing good and evil" (Genesis 3:5). Satan didn't lie when he made this statement. Indeed, the tree was called the tree of the knowledge of good and evil, and when Adam and Eve ate the fruit from it, God said, "The man has now become like one of us, knowing good and evil" (3:22).

So when man followed the advice of Satan, he gained powers he previously did not possess. What Satan didn't tell him was that he was not equipped to live with this knowledge. Man's first insight from his newly claimed powers was the fact that he was naked. Self-centeredness had been born. Man could no longer look at his mate with the same selfless acceptance he had always had before. Both man and woman, self-conscious in their newborn attitudes toward one another, hastened to cover their bodies.

Self-centeredness gave birth to guilt, and this guilt estranged man from himself, from others, and from God. When God called to Adam and Eve after they had sinned, Adam replied, "I heard you . . . and I was afraid because I was naked; so I hid" (3:10). Guilt alienates. "I was afraid." Adam was the first neurotic.

As children of Adam, we continue to bear the burden of our knowledge of good and evil. "The requirements of the law are written on their hearts, their consciences also bearing witness . . . accusing . . . defending . . ." (Romans 2:15). Here is another characteristic we can count on being present in the hearts of those to whom we are sent. Because man knows right from wrong, his conscience prods him incessantly with feelings of guilt.

Man experiences futility. Another effect of the fall is man's sense of futility. God said, "Cursed is the ground because of you; through painful toil you will eat of it all the days of your life. It will produce thorns and thistles for you. . . . By the sweat of your brow you will eat your food until you return to the ground" (Genesis 3:17-19). In other words, life is a struggle—a rather pointless struggle. We expend our lives just managing to exist. Then it is back to dust.

The things we plan and look forward to with anticipation never quite measure up to our expectations. They keep coming up "thorns and thistles." We marry the person of our dreams, and then the marriage falls apart. We look forward to having children, and then they break our hearts. We sacrifice and study to become established in a profession, and then we discover our work to be tedious. So we look forward to retirement. And on and on it goes.

Due to the fall, life is a struggle against desperation. Probably all of us can identify to some degree with the words of the first existentialist to go on record: "What does a man get for all the toil and anxious striving with which he labors under the sun? All his days his work is pain and grief; even at night his mind does not rest. This too is meaningless" (Ecclesiastes 2:22-23).

Has a person ever lived who has not stopped to ask the existential question, "Why am I doing all this?" only to carry on with the question unanswered and the course of his life unaltered?

This struggle against futility is something God brought upon man. Consequently, it must have a positive function within God's purposes. God expelled man from paradise and plunged him into this struggle, not out of a desire for revenge but out of love. In paradise there is no pain. Those feelings of futility are a gift from God. Without them, who would seek reconciliation? This, too, works toward the progress of the gospel in people's hearts.

Man experiences death. Man's persistence to survive, his perseverance in the face of the absurdity of it all, is another part of the riddle of man. The first clues to this phenomenon are also found in man's fall.

At the fall, man died. He died in every sense of the word. He died in his relationship to God, in his relationship to his fellow man, and in his relationship to himself. Spiritually, it was sudden death. His physical death was slower. We spend years dying. Guilt eats away at our health. The psalmist laments, "There is no health in my body; my bones have no soundness because of my sin. My guilt has overwhelmed me like a burden too heavy to bear" (Psalm 38:3-4).

Why does man resist death the way he does? Why is he so obsessively fearful of it? The Bible says that Satan holds the power of death and that man is held in slavery by his fear of death (Hebrews 2:14-15). Death is an enemy that man will do anything to fight off to preserve his futile existence. Why?

I think it is because man instinctively subscribes to his own uniqueness. Although he may consciously disclaim beliefs to this effect, he is normally unwilling to give up on life until he has done his best to live out this uniqueness. He just cannot make peace with the idea that seventy years is all there is.

God has "set eternity in the hearts of men; yet they cannot fathom what God has done from beginning to end" (Ecclesiastes 3:11). So there lies within man a drive for immortality. This drive is often expressed in bizarre ways. The Egyptian Pharaohs devoted their lives to building their own tombs. This drive is another characteristic that people hold in common, a drive that makes them susceptible to spiritual things.

We observed earlier that communication must begin from a common ground—something the communicator and the receiver mutually understand. Human beings by nature hold a number of characteristics in common. The individual person knows that he is unique, that he is restless, and that he cannot accept the fact of his own mortality. This is man—as he has always been and as he will always be. Times and cultures cannot eliminate these primal drives.

So there does exist a positive common ground. We *can* communicate spiritual truth. Man *can* understand and respond because God has sown certain things in his heart. I think this is what the apostle John was desribing when he said that Jesus was "the true light that gives light to every man" (John 1:9).

MAN IS INFLUENCED BY HIS SOCIETY.

There is a third major factor that affects the make-up of the people of our times. Rather than unifying, however, this factor differentiates and separates people into cultures and even generations. It is the factor of *environment.*

The Old Testament warnings to Israel upon entering the land of Canaan attest to the reality of this factor. "You must not do as they do in Egypt, where you used to live, and you must not do as they do in the land of Canaan, where I am bringing you" (Leviticus 18:3).

In the same vein, Paul warns Christians in his letter to the Romans, "Do not conform any longer to the pattern of this world" (Romans 12:2).

Man is highly susceptible to being conditioned by whatever society he happens to be a part of—inescapably so. Countless studies have been made and volumes have been written in the field of psychology on environmental influences. It would be beside the point for us to develop a long discussion on the subject here. Rather, let's begin with the assumption that mas is influenced by his environment and that this influence is fundamental to the shaping of a person's ethics, values, and world view.

The clearest illustrations of this assumption are found in the differences that exist between peoples of different cultures. Anthropologist Edward Hall observes, "Any Westerner who was raised outside the Far East and claims he really understands and can communicate with either the Chinese or the Japanese is deluding himself."[5] The differences wrought by environment are real and cannot be ignored if understanding is to exist.

It is intriguing that people are so susceptible to being conditioned by their society. True, most of the process is subliminal, but this tremendous susceptibility raises a question. What is it about man that allows him to blindly embrace the values and characteristics of those that surround him, even when those values are obviously irrational and destructive? Can this not be traced back to man's fallen nature? In Romans 1 we are told that when men cut themselves loose from God to strike out on their own, they lose the ability to reason properly. "Although they knew God, they neither glorified him as God nor gave thanks to him, but their thinking became futile and their foolish hearts were darkened. Although they claimed to be wise, they became fools" (1:21-22).

Man's mind is a good tool for small projects but is often inadequate for large-scale matters. Man is a subjective creature. Consequently, his beliefs and values are, in the main, acquired on the subconscious level.

The important point here is that man tends to unquestioningly embrace the prevailing values of his generation. Although we are inescapably children of our times, often the values of the times are radically different from biblical values. The commonalities that bond us together as human beings are so deeply buried that they are almost invisible.

In 1979 a study was done among teenagers in Sweden, who were asked to respond to the statement, "I think the following could give my life more meaning. . . ." Of those surveyed, 87 percent thought that meaning could be found in a good job, 85 percent thought it could be found in a marriage partner, and 84 percent thought it could be found in sports and recreation. Only 15 percent thought that quiet time and prayer could help, and another 15 percent indicated that they thought alcohol could help.

About 80 percent considered the question of the meaning of life important, yet 80 percent considered it unimportant whether Jesus existed as a man on earth or not. Also, 85 percent considered it unimportant whether Jesus is the Son of God or not. A full 75 percent concluded that the question of God's existence is unimportant.[6]

My experience indicates that this survey is representative of the prevailing values of our times. Because there are similar tendencies throughout Western Europe and many parts of the United States, it appears that this generation is giving up on traditional religious explanations. Although the question of the meaning of life is considered important, people are basically unconcerned about the existence of either God or Jesus. Jesus, whoever He was, is now considered irrelevant. Self-satisfaction and immediate concerns— job, girlfriend or boyfriend, and skiing—are the important things. Although this tendency is taking place in the mainstream of our society, it is often unobserved by people who are thoroughly immersed in the Christian counterculture without close relationships with people of this generation.

AN EXERCISE IN EMPATHY

Let's imagine for a moment that we have just described you! You, as a child of the times, have given up on looking for religious answers to life. It just doesn't occur to you to think about God or Jesus Christ. You see them as part of the rubble of the crumbled institutions of previous generations. Life is important to you, but you have concluded that there is only seventy years of it and nothing beyond.

The years have gone by. Today is your fortieth birthday. That in itself represents a major crisis. You are no longer "in your thirties"—you are *forty!* Life is important to you. Since seventy years is all you have, you realize that sixty percent of your life is gone. It's time to reevaluate things.

You look in the mirror and, sure enough, you're slipping. The hairline, the extra pounds, the little creases that promise wrinkles to come. Your two children are teenagers who have clearly communicated that they feel parents are an unnecessary complication in their lives. Your career is set. You know you will never be very rich, very famous, or very influential.

Now you have just gotten up in the morning and these are the first thoughts running through your mind. How are you going to react? You'll think, "Life is getting away from me! I've got to make the most of it—enjoy it more. That's it!"

But how are you going to do that? How will this resolution make this day any different? Within your existential frame of reference, what is important? What is there to look forward to, to give yourself to? Not much. Perhaps a good cup of coffee, a walk in the park, or an extramarital affair— whatever feels good to the senses. But whatever you find to do, it will be accompanied by a sense of loss when you realize that another day is gone.

This little scenario highlights the practical difference between the Christian and the nonChristian. The difference is one of *hope.* Ephesians 2:12 says, "You were separate from Christ . . . without hope and without God in the world."

The Christian and the nonChristian function according to two different value systems. The scope of the life view of the Christian embraces eternity, while the nonChristian lives merely for his seventy years. The enormous distance between these two perspectives results in differences of equal magnitude in the things to which we attach value in our everyday lives.

Projecting yourself one more time into our scenario, one question remains: What do you think it would take to awaken your interest in the Christian message, to induce you to go back and examine it, having already discarded it as an unimportant relic? What would it take for a ray of hope to penetrate the accumulated layers of disenchantment?

NOTES
1. Arnold Toynbee, *Mankind and Mother Earth* (Paladin, Great Britain: Granada Publishing, 1978), page 2.
2. Toynbee, page 2.
3. Toynbee, page 2.
4. Toynbee, page 3.
5. Edward Hall, *Beyond Culture* (Garden City, New York: Anchor Press, Doubleday, 1976), page 2.
6. Rinus Baljeu, "Evangelism: Secularization and The Navigators," (August 1982), Appendix: Diagrams 6 and 7.

3

Jesus and the People of His Generation

Contemporary man is remarkably blind, irrational, and highly susceptible to the conditioning of his culture. The institutions of his society are deliberately influencing him to conclude that theistic religious belief is superstition; that liberation and integrity lie in acknowledging the relative nature of truth; that it is somehow noble to live with the ensuing struggle against futility.

How do we as Christians, carrying the Great Commission in our hearts, respond to this adverse indoctrination? It is so easy to become intimidated, to feel incompetent in the face of the disparity between the Christian and secular positions. Who, we ask, is competent to mount a counterattack?

There may be an unusual person here and there who is equal to the challenge, but we are quite sure that it is not us.

So the temptation to give up, to direct our efforts toward those with whom we feel more comfortable, is almost overwhelming. But we are mistaken. It is not that difficult. It is within the capacity of the average Christian to be effective among the people of this generation. Because we are sent to *every* creature, we can hardly conclude that the mainstream of our society is out of reach!

THERE IS ONLY ONE ISSUE.

The apostle John began his Gospel by describing Jesus as the light of the world. The theme of light and darkness runs throughout the entire book. Such a theme is worthy of our scrutiny because it is the biblical response to the problems of man we have just addressed.

Jesus stated clearly that He is the light that man needs: "I have come into the world as a light, so that no one who believes in me should stay in darkness" (John 12:46).

Now this is good news for darkened minds! And this is *our* message, too. It is the only message we have, because He is the only true light. Our singular objective must be to communicate Jesus Christ.

You may feel that this is a lot easier said than done. Did we not just recognize that those we seek to win don't even care if Jesus existed or if He was who He claimed to be? Since they don't care, how can we expect a response when we approach them with the news that Jesus is the light of the world?

But the fact remains, He *is* the light; there isn't any other. If any ray of hope is to penetrate the thinking of this generation, it is going to be this ray. Impossible? Jesus faced a similar situation. Let's take a close look at the basis of Jesus' communication with the people of His generation.

JESUS, THE UNIVERSAL TRUTH

The people in Jesus' life can be divided into four categories: the multitudes, His enemies, His disciples, and the Twelve. There is one theme that remains constant in His communication with each of these four groups. Because of this consistency and because of the nature of this theme, we can conclude that we are dealing with a universal truth. It is timeless in its significance and in its effectiveness.

This universal truth, when given its proper prominence and offered without adulteration, penetrates to the core, for it appeals to the essential and unchanging nature of man. As it unfolds, even those we regard as the least likely often begin to respond to God's call to enter His kingdom.

Jesus and His Opponents. What was the root issue that put Jesus' adversaries into conflict with Him? Jesus identified it in John 8:23-25: "You are from below; I am from above. You are of this world; I am not of this world. . . . If you do not believe that I am the one I claim to be, you will indeed die in your sins."

"Who are you?" they asked. That is the question! The essential issue of every relationship in Jesus' life dealt with the question of His identity. It is still the foremost question. *Who is Jesus?*

When a mortal man claims he is deity, honest intellectual questions are certainly in order! Jesus clearly claimed to be God, but the fascinating thing about the dialogues between Jesus and His accusers was that the debate never centered on the intellectual tenability of that claim. Almost without exception the thrust of the dialogue was a focus on the overly subjective nature of their resistance against Him.

OBSTACLES TO FAITH—Jesus encountered many people who were unwilling to follow Him because of certain areas of resistance in their lives. Those who try to evangelize others still encounter these obstacles to faith.

1. *Public opinion*—On one occasion Jesus asked the Jews who opposed Him, "How can you believe if you accept praise from one another?" (John 5:44). He was attempting to show them that it was their *concern for their own social status* that was barring the way.

2. *Misinformation*—On another occasion a discussion broke out among the people surrounding Jesus over this issue of His identity (John 7:40-42). "Some of the people said, 'Surely this man is the Prophet.' Others said, 'He is the Christ.' Still others asked, 'How can the Christ come from Galilee? Does not the Scripture say that the Christ will come from David's family and from Bethlehem?'"

In this case the obstacle was *misinformation*. The things people thought they knew—casually formed, preconceived notions—got in the way of true understanding.

3. *Self-sufficiency*—Later, Jesus was conversing with a man He had just healed who had been blind from birth (John 9:35-41). The subject was the same! "Do you believe in the Son of Man?" Jesus asked.

"Who is he, sir?" asked the blind man. Jesus said, "He is the one speaking with you." Then the man acknowledged his faith in Jesus.

With that, Jesus addressed the crowd: "For judgment I have come into this world, so that the blind will see and those who see will become blind." The Pharisees in the crowd got the point and asked, "What? Are we blind too?" Jesus replied that they were, in fact, blind. Because they insisted that they could see, they were blind to their own spiritual blindness.

In this situation the obstacle was *man's excessive faith in himself.* These presumptuous Pharisees felt they had it within themselves to work their way spiritually through life on their own.

Again, the barrier was not due to lack of knowledge; it was due to an excess of subjectivity.

4. *Concern for position*—Irrationality growing out of subjectivity apparently knows no limits. The case of Lazarus demonstrates this fact clearly (John 11:1-12:11). As in almost every other situation, Jesus used a crisis to focus on the critical issue of His identity.

Imagine the scene: Lazarus is dead. We spent all night at the wake. Then Jesus appears. By now He is enormously famous for His sayings and His miracles. But now He performs a miracle unlike any other—He raises Lazarus from the dead! How do you react to this? Do you conclude that Jesus is God?

Amazingly, the reaction of some is, "If we let him go on like this, everyone will believe in him." So what's wrong with that? "Then the Romans will come and take away both our place and our nation" (11:48).

Position, prestige, the status quo—all take priority over truth in the value system of most people.

So how did those who opposed Jesus handle truth? They tried to eliminate it! The Sanhedrin passed the death sentence on Jesus and, furthermore, "the chief priests made plans to kill Lazarus as well" (12:10). Irrational men! If they can't refute the evidence, they destroy it!

5. *Rebellion*—Finally, it was this issue of Jesus' identity that cost Him His life (Matthew 26:63-68). At His trial, "The high priest said to him, 'I charge you under oath by the living God: Tell us if you are the Christ, the Son of God.' 'Yes, it is as you say,' Jesus replied." With that they declared Him worthy of death.

There is a demanding logic that leads to this irrational rejection of Jesus' claim to deity: To acknowledge that Jesus is God is to acknowledge He is authority, and to acknowledge His authority is to acknowledge His right to authority over me. *Rebellion* is the fundamental problem of mankind from the time of the fall. To concede to His deity without submitting to His authority is to acknowledge that rebellion. This is a very difficult concession for any individual to make. In the final analysis, rebellion is always the real issue.

Jesus and the Multitudes. On the surface, the response of the multitudes to Jesus was almost the opposite from that of His religious enemies. The multitudes liked Jesus. They followed Him everywhere He went. They were much like the religious people of our day. To them, it was important to have a faith. It gives structure to life, and, besides, children need to be raised with some solid moral principles. But often their true response was identical to the response of those who were openly opposed to Him.

Two things attracted the multitudes to Jesus: (1) They were amazed at His teaching, "because he taught them as one who had authority, not as the teachers of the law"; and (2) they were amazed at His power: "He even gives orders to evil spirits and they obey him" (Mark 1:22,27). Jesus was fun to be around. He was fun to listen to and fun to watch.

Jesus' popularity grew to the extent that on certain occasions "so many gathered that there was no room left, not even outside the door. . . . A crowd gathered, so that he and his disciples were not even able to eat" (Mark 2:2, 3:20-21). Jesus' family became so concerned for Him that they felt compelled "to take charge of him." They thought He had gone out of His mind!

Jesus was famous. He by far eclipsed John the Baptist. Everyone was euphoric about Him—*the multitudes,* who enjoyed everything about Jesus, and *the twelve disciples,* who basked in the reflection of His popularity. But Jesus was not impressed. In fact, He eventually put an end to it all.

On one occasion, Jesus confronted those who were

following Him with the fact that He was dissatisfied with their response to Him. He said, "You are looking for me . . . because you ate the loaves and had your fill. Do not work for food that spoils, but for food that endures to eternal life." They asked, "What must we do to do the works God requires?" Jesus answered, "The work of God is this: to believe in the one he has sent" (John 6:26-29).

Again the issue was that of His identity. Jesus was essentially saying, "You are following Me for pragmatic reasons, but that is not good enough. If you are going to follow Me, it must be on My terms—and those terms are to accept Me as God!"

The people understood what He was saying, but they revealed their unbelief with their response, "What miraculous sign then will you give that we may see it and believe you? What will you do?" (6:30).

Unbelievable! They had seen Him cast out demons, heal the sick, and feed the multitudes. They had marveled at His teachings. They could accept Him as a great teacher, as a miracle worker, as a prophet, or as a political leader, but to accept Him as God was just asking too much!

Jesus, knowing this, sent them on their way with a few incisive, difficult statements about Himself: "I am the bread of life. . . . I have come down from heaven. . . . This bread is my flesh. . . . Unless you eat the flesh of the Son of Man and drink his blood, you have no life in you" (John 6:35,38,51,53).

The multitude reacted immediately. The people grumbled among themselves. They argued, they complained, and they were offended. "From this time many of his disciples turned back and no longer followed him" (6:66).

At any given point in this discussion, Jesus could have eased up, but He knew what He was doing. He was deliberately dividing the people . . . with this issue of His identity. In essence, He was saying, "Either believe that I am who I am, accepting all the implications, or go back to your homes! Stop deluding yourselves by following Me around!"

Why was it so hard for the people to accept those conditions? They seemed to be coming along so well! But it was here that they revealed how very similar they were to those who were Jesus' openly avowed enemies. Why is it so hard to acknowledge Jesus' identity? It is because we can't both be in control. There can only be one king! It is so hard to give up our ill-fitting sovereignty.

Jesus and His Disciples. This same thread—Jesus' identity—runs through everything He taught His disciples. In fact, Jesus apparently reserved most of His teachings of any significance for those of His followers who committed themselves to the truth of His identity. He spoke in parables and in enigmatic terms to the multitudes. It is clear that they understood very little. Jesus said to His disciples, "The secret of the kingdom of God has been given to you. But to those on the outside everything is said in parables so that, 'they may be ever seeing but never perceiving'" (Mark 4:11-12).

What was happening here? Was Jesus deliberately withholding truth from hungry people? Not at all! The Bible goes on to explain, "With many similar parables Jesus spoke the word to them, *as much as they could understand.* He did not say anything to them [the multitudes] without using a parable. But when he was alone with his own disciples, he explained everything" (Mark 4:33-34).

Jesus taught the multitudes all He could, which wasn't much, because they had rejected His divine identity, the very basis of most theological truth. Until we embrace the foremost premise of Jesus' teachings—that He is God—none of the rest is going to make much sense.

Jesus broadened the disciples' understanding of the -dimensions of His authority. His authority, too, is rooted in

His identity—who He is. Jesus displayed His authority over human authorities (Mark 1:22), over Satan (Mark 1:27), over sin (Mark 2:9), over creation (Mark 2:10), over tradition (Mark 2:27-28), and even over life and death (John 10:18, 19:10-11). In short, His response to His disciples over the question "Who am I?" was essentially "I am authority over everything in heaven and on earth."

A true disciple understands the dimensions of Christ's authority and brings his life step by step under that authority. As he does this, something miraculous takes place. His bondage is replaced by freedom (John 8:31-32). He overcomes the world. This is a critical truth. Jesus says to everyone, "What is your problem? Whatever it is, give it to Me, because I have destroyed the power of that particular problem. I have authority over that one. Leave it with Me. I will resolve it and you can go free."

Making disciples is helping someone else experience and understand the dynamics of Christ's authority so that he, too, can go free. Here again, Jesus' identity is the determinative issue. For Jesus' opponents and for the multitudes who followed Him, the question of His identity determined life and death. For His disciples it determined freedom and bondage. But what about the twelve men who stayed close to Him for three years?

Jesus and the Twelve. In the training of the Twelve, Jesus carried the issue of His identity to its ultimate implications. That this issue was, in fact, central to everything He did with the Twelve is demonstrated in His prayer to the Father in John 17.

He began this prayer by underscoring the centrality of His identity to His entire ministry. "Now this is eternal life: that they [all believers] may know you [the Father], the only true God, and Jesus Christ, whom you have sent" (17:3).

Then He went on to intercede for the Twelve. "I have revealed you to those whom you gave me out of the world. . . . They knew with certainty that I came from you, and they believed that you sent me" (17:6-8). The training of the Twelve consisted of bringing those men into a firsthand acquaintance with God and into a comprehension that Jesus and the Father are one and the same God! Jesus said, "If you really knew me, you would know my Father as well. From now on, you do know him and have seen him. . . . Anyone who has seen me has seen the Father" (John 14:7, 9).

Jesus spent most of His short time of ministry communicating this single fact to His small handful of men: He and His Father are one. To grasp the implications of what this unity means is to understand the basis of all spiritual power (John 14:20). As Jesus said, "Apart from me you can do nothing. . . . [But with me you] will do even greater things than [my miracles], because I am going to the Father" (John 15:5, 14:12).

If Jesus had not left behind Him men who were gripped by this understanding of His identity, there would have been no future for the Christian movement. Jesus said, "All authority in heaven and on earth has been given to me. *Therefore* go and make disciples of all nations" (Matthew 28:18-19). A full comprehension and acceptance of Jesus' identity makes us full participants of His power. The Great Commission would have been a fool's errand with anything less.

The continuity of this theme of Jesus' identity as it runs through all His relationships demonstrates that it is an issue of ultimate importance! Every other theme is subordinate to this one. *He* is the gospel. *He* is our message. Everything else we Christians believe and hold dear is an outworking of this one truth. If we are to be effective among the people of this generation, this fact of His identity must be very clear in our minds.

4

The Message for Our Generation

The divine identity of Jesus must be the substance of our evangelism. Since He considered it vitally important to concentrate on the fact and implications of His identity, we would be well advised to put forth the same emphasis. In this chapter we will identify some of the ways in which we unwittingly blur this focus on Christ.

THE GOSPEL OF POPULAR ISSUES

What is the gospel? This is a question theologians and Christian leaders love to ask. Usually when they pose it the implication is that no one within earshot has the faintest notion of the answer. I usually come away from such dialogues with feelings of frustration.

And yet I've observed something quite significant in these discussions. Almost always when this question of the gospel is posed, the questioner has an ulterior motive. He really wants to make us guess what *his* particular gospel happens to be. It is the gospel—plus his emphasis! For example, one of the big issues today is that of social justice. So the gospel according to one questioner might be a gospel of social justice. For another, it might be a gospel of prosperity. For another, it might be a gospel of civil rights.

The process is simple. We focus on an issue that so impresses us that it looms in our minds as *the* issue of utmost importance. Then we proceed to make that issue or truth an essential part of our message. When we do that, we create a partisan gospel. We use Jesus to support our private cause. He becomes the Jesus of the poor, or the Jesus of women's rights, or the Jesus of whatever other issue happens to be front page at the moment. But a partisan Jesus cannot also be a universal Jesus.

THE GOSPEL OF OUR PERSONAL EMPHASIS

Most of us emphasize certain doctrines far more than others. We favor certain forms of expressing our faith because they are so natural to us that we can't envision a Christian functioning without them. Often we consider certain behavior to be normative and essential. Our strong feelings prompt us to elevate or to emphasize these ideas to the point where they become requirements for anyone we minister to.

This tendency restricts the gospel. We need to be careful of our religious traditions, our forms of worship, our personal doctrinal emphases—anything that is not in balance with the whole of Scripture. If we are not in balance, then we offer a

Jesus who is identified with things that may be important to us but are a stumbling block to those we seek to win. They won't take Him because of the wrappings.

THE GOSPEL AND OUR ECCLESIASTICAL SYSTEMS

Which Jesus Christ are the Swedish youth rejecting? The Christ of the Reformation, of the Free Church, or of the Roman Catholic Church? Almost certainly it is one of these, but probably not the *real* Christ. In the reality of His fullness, Jesus cannot be confined to any system. Did He become a Protestant with the Reformation? Was He ever a Roman Catholic? Rather, He stands above our ecclesiastical structures and our theological systems. He is the gospel focus of all time, for all peoples. When we identify Him with our particular ecclesiastical persuasion, we isolate Him in a limited sphere. In the process, we exclude much of the rest of the world.

I once spent several days teaching the Bible to some Christian friends who had lived in Communist bloc countries. These Christian brothers had spent the last thirty-five years concentrating on survival. Preservation had taken priority over outreach, and understandably so. In this situation the Church moves toward isolationism by necessity. Legalism is almost inevitable under such circumstances. Because many Christians in Communist countries have begun to realize that this process of excessive narrowness has occurred, they are now taking steps to strike a better balance.

As I read Scriptures concerning the freedom we have in Christ, one woman burst out, "If this is true, then there is hope for my parents! They can be won! Until now I thought they could come to Christ only if they would join the Baptist Church!"

A Baptist Jesus!

THE GOSPEL OF THE CHRISTIAN CONTRACT

Possibly the most common weakness in our contemporary approaches to evangelism is our tendency to focus our message on the Christian contract—how to transact a relationship with God—rather than on the person of Jesus Christ. We become so intent on helping someone understand how to put his faith in Christ that we overlook the very real probability that he is almost devoid in his knowledge of Christ.

It is far wiser to focus on Jesus Christ than on the contract. Instead of telling people what they need to do, we want to bring them into an understanding of who Jesus is. As this understanding grows, the response—what the person needs to do—becomes self-evident. I have found that, more often than not, when the truth about Christ is fully understood, the response occurs without my help.

This preoccupation with the contract rather than with the person of Christ creates another weakness in our evangelism. We tend to become more interested in responses than in *understanding*. We strive to elicit agreement, and once it is achieved we seek to extract a positive response. We call this "making a decision." This is the forced contract.

Too often this kind of contract is little more than leading a person to verbalize certain phrases that we suggest to him. Once he makes the right sounds, we think he is "saved."

THE GOSPEL OF JESUS CHRIST

The gospel *is* Jesus Christ, who died, was buried, and then rose again and ascended to the Father. He is nonpartisan, standing above our human structures and our secondary issues. If we expect to communicate with the people of this generation, we must allow Jesus His rightful universality. We must offer an unencumbered Christ.

Twenty years ago we were beginning our ministry in Brazil. We found ourselves in circumstances that led us to challenge many convictions we had previously embraced without reservation. The students with whom we were working were not responsive to the gospel we were preaching. The barriers were the result of some of the secondary elements we had added to the gospel, plus the fact that we represented something institutional and foreign to them. We weren't presenting an unadorned Jesus.

In this context, we began to understand that our gospel message should be Jesus, and nothing else. We are not sent to defend or promote economic or political systems, religious structures, or our own organization. Our message is that of a Person, and we are not free to represent Him with encumbrances. We realized that we are called to impose no human standards, to honor no traditions. We are called to proclaim Jesus, no strings attached.

When we got that clear, we quickly discovered that we had positive communication with the same kind of people who had previously been keeping us at arm's length. We began to reap a harvest that continues to this day.

This approach to the gospel is so basic and simple. Who is Jesus? Take a look for yourself. If you don't believe, we understand that. But let's go to the Bible with this single question in order to research the answer. You don't accept the Bible? We understand that, too. We begin on this basis— and count on Christ's superiority to accomplish the rest.

TRUST IN THE SUPERIORITY OF CHRIST

Francisco is one of my dearest friends. When we met a few years ago, he was an agnostic emerging from years of Marxism. He had probably never looked inside a Bible, and yet one evening he showed up at a Bible study I was leading.

Francisco is from northeast Brazil, an impoverished area that frequently passes through long periods of drought. Having been raised in poverty, Francisco was motivated to revolt against the system that seems to perpetuate destitution. At eight years of age he declared he would become a medical doctor, and he also decided he would have nothing to do with the Church. For him, God didn't exist. Gifted with unusual intelligence and fortitude, Francisco kept his word.

Years later he was on a surgical team with a Christian friend of mine. God used this friend to awaken Francisco's interest in spiritual things. It was a word here and there, often in a joking manner, often during the course of surgery.

Circumstances of various sorts began to close in on Francisco—family, patients, and others. Francisco decided that my friend was right: He needed to give attention to the spiritual side of life. With typical perseverance he set out to do this. "The spiritual must be related to spiritism," he reasoned. So he enrolled in a yearlong orientation course at a spiritist center, and began to study the occult. He kept this fact to himself. Eventually, my friend enticed Francisco to visit our Bible study.

Because Francisco was fascinated by the Bible, he absorbed it avidly. He brought his wife with him the second week, and from then on they never missed.

Three months went by, during which we were greatly encouraged by Francisco's and Danelia's progress toward Christ. Then one day he came to discuss "a special situation" with me. My heart sank as I learned of their involvement with the spiritists. They had been in the course for six months, and he felt he needed to honor his word, following through to the end. He told me that he'd already been offered the position of teacher in a new center but that he hadn't accepted it yet.

As I sat there, my mind raced through the passages in the Old and New Testaments that treat this subject of spiritism.

There are enough verses for an overkill, and my first impulse was to use them all. But when you are unsure of a person's exact relationship with Christ, a scriptural deluge can be fatal to the person's further response. I held my tongue.

Finally I said, "Francisco, I'd like to show you something." We turned to 1 John 4 and I asked him to read the first few verses to me: "Dear friends, do not believe every spirit, but test the spirits to see whether they are from God. . . . This is how you can recognize the Spirit of God: Every spirit that acknowledges that Jesus Christ has come in the flesh is from God, but every spirit that does not acknowledge Jesus is not from God."

I went on to explain, "You are receiving information from two different sources, from me and from the spiritist center. Both of us claim to be teaching the truth. Both talk a lot about Jesus. According to this passage, by what criteria will you evaluate and decide who is, in fact, teaching you the truth?"

I continued, "I have a suggestion. When you go to the center, listen very carefully to what they say about Jesus, and then compare that with what the Bible says. Do the same with me. Compare what you hear me say about Jesus with what the Bible says. Then decide who's right on the basis of this passage."

When Francisco left that day, I was very apprehensive. I was aware of the hold spiritism can so easily gain over an individual. And I wasn't even sure Francisco had come far enough to where the Scriptures were authority for him.

But Francisco did what I told him, and it wasn't long before his new birth became evident. The final day of the course at the spiritist center came along. They renewed their offer for him to become a teacher. But he replied, "Thank you very much for the time and attention you invested in me. It has been interesting and informative. But I have also been studying the Bible. I've concluded that the Jesus you present is not the Jesus of the Bible. There is no salvation in your Jesus." And with that he left them. The superiority of Jesus!

OUR ROLE IN EVANGELISM

Our message is the good news about a person, for the gospel lies in the person of Jesus. Christianity and Jesus are not the same. People may have Him without embracing the systems that have been built up around Him. Or they can be involved in the system without knowing anything about Him. Whoever receives Him must take Him on His terms. To have Him at all is to take all of Him. Because He is sovereign over all that exists, He is sovereign over my person. This is the gospel in its essence.

Our role in evangelism can be compared with what John the Baptist said about himself. He saw himself as the best man in the wedding. Jesus is the bridegroom. The one who hears and believes is the bride. John's job was to see to it that the marriage occurred successfully, without attracting attention to himself in the process. The bride doesn't take on the best man's name. She belongs to the bridegroom.

When we understand that our intent in presenting the gospel is to bring about a new marriage, the secularized of this generation suddenly seem much closer. They are within reach. Of course, some, even after taking an honest look, will turn Jesus down. We cannot prevent that. But we *can* do something about people who reject Him because He comes wrapped in the traditions, dogmas, or moralisms of the messenger. Such potentially damaging influences we can avoid.

We must always remember that evangelism is not merely presenting the terms of a contract. It is introducing the person of Jesus Christ. It is taking the time to help a person grasp the implications of His identity.

Evangelism is not merely bringing a person to intellectual assent; it goes beyond that. It includes helping a person work his way through his own rebellion or volitional obstacles.

For secularized people this whole issue of Jesus' identity is not a concern. Nobody is asking the question. So how do I get a person to become interested in researching an answer to a question to which he is indifferent? It will take the rest of this book to answer that one!

PART TWO

A Practical Guide for Lifestyle Evangelism

Introduction

By far the most frequent question that arises regarding evangelism has to do with how to awaken interest in secular people. How do we approach evangelism among people in the mainstream? The subject of religion is not at all included among the concerns of secularized people. Thus, how to awaken interest among the uninterested is the first question in evangelism!

Then as we actually become involved in the lives of our nonChristian friends, a myriad of other how-to questions quickly surface. We discover that methods and explanations that were once effective simply no longer communicate. So there is a perpetual need for new methods and approaches that correspond to the changing mentality of society.

It is vitally important to have right methods, for they serve as our tools. But it would be misleading to give the impression that effectiveness is simply a matter of right tactics. There are two other factors that are even more fundamental: (1) We need an accompanying change of mind-set and (2) We need to be dependent on spiritual resources, not on techniques.

CHANGING OUR MIND-SET

Cultural shifts produce deep changes in world views and values. For this reason we need to learn to be cross-cultural missionaries right on our own block! Communication depends on our understanding of the people we go to. This understanding is accomplished as we put ourselves in the other's shoes for the sake of seeing life from his perspective. This is what it means to change one's mind-set. It involves undergoing a change in our own thinking. Thus we come to understand and empathize with the other's value system. This cultural insight becomes the footing for the bridge that will span the distance between them and Jesus Christ.

RELYING ON SPIRITUAL RESOURCES

Probably the most dangerous thing about methods is that when they work we begin to rely on them. We experiment with something. It works. We do it again, and again it works. As we become successful, we slip into thinking that continued success is a matter of just keeping that activity going. We feel that if we just repeat it long enough and hard enough, we will accomplish our goals. But when we transfer our confidence to such success-formula approaches, we are also resorting to carnal weaponry.

Our primary spiritual resources are the Spirit of God and the Word of God. Any true progress, any real spiritual victory, is gained through the power of these two forces.

THE METAMORPHOSIS FROM SAUL TO PAUL

The apostle Paul's experience of shedding his past to become the first apostle to the Gentiles is an illustration of the power of the Spirit of God and the Word of God in a person's life. Paul had to undergo a metamorphosis of his mind-set, learning to rely on spiritual resources.

Paul began his ministry immediately after his conversion. He had all the qualifications for success. After all, he was a ranking Pharisee, schooled under Gamaliel. If anybody had the potential to be effective among the Jews, Paul did. In Damascus where he was converted, he immediately began to unleash his impressive powers on the Jewish community. "Saul grew more and more powerful and baffled the Jews living in Damascus by proving that Jesus is the Christ" (Acts 9:22).

Paul seemed to win every argument. But rather than inspiring belief, he inspired his hearers to wrath. They wanted to kill him! He escaped Damascus in a basket.

In Jerusalem Paul again showed himself to be an invincible debater, but with similar results. So "the brothers . . . took him down to Caesarea and sent him off to Tarsus. Then the church throughout Judea, Galilee and Samaria enjoyed a time of peace" (Acts 9:30-31). Perhaps there was a connection between Paul's departure and the ensuing peace!

As Paul departed for Tarsus, he might have considered his encounters in Damascus and Jerusalem as a double failure. But according to him those failures were some of the most significant experiences of his action-packed life (2 Corinthians 11:30-33). Failure is usually a very effective teacher, especially when under the guidance of God.

In the following years, alone with God, the Scriptures, and his own thoughts, Paul underwent a transformation. When he returned he was a different man with apparently a different kind of approach. Laying aside all carnal resources, the transformed apostle resolved to approach the ministry with exclusively spiritual weaponry (see 2 Corinthians 10:3-4).

Here is how Paul described his way of presenting the gospel after the change: "I did not come with *eloquence* or *superior wisdom.* . . . For I resolved to know nothing while I was with you except Jesus Christ and him crucified. . . . My message and my preaching were not with *wise and persuasive words* . . . so that your faith might not rest on men's wisdom" (1 Corinthians 2:1-5).

What constituted carnal weapons for Paul? Eloquence, superior wisdom, and wise and persuasive words! Although he was a natural at using all three, laying them aside was a deliberate decision, something he "resolved" to do.

Apparently during that time when Paul was alone with his thoughts, God impressed upon him the fact that the knowledge he possessed and the prestige he enjoyed were not what people needed from him. He would have felt more secure had he continued to operate from his own natural strengths and advantages. But he set them aside, and, instead, with fear and trembling he came in at the hearer's level of need.

THE BEST METHODS ARE YOUR OWN.

Methods in and of themselves have inherent limitations. A method is normally born in an attempt to meet a local need within a given set of circumstances. Then the word gets around and others begin to use that proven method. But as its use is extended to other situations, its effectiveness is limited to the degree of similarity between the two environments. Therefore, I do not intend to set forth "a method" on the following pages. Rather, my purpose is to offer principles and examples that will stimulate new ideas. Creativity involves the ability to see new combinations between things that are already familiar.

You will need methods. If you take any methods from these pages, be sure to adapt them to your own situation. The result should be uniquely your own.

5
Evangelism Is a Team Effort

You want to be involved in evangelism. You would hardly be reading this page in this book at this moment if that weren't the case. Let's say you are sufficiently motivated to be willing to commit yourself to action. What should your very first step be? I would suggest that it be to find at least one kindred spirit, one other individual who shares that same desire, and commit yourselves to working together.

Surprising? Perhaps, but it shouldn't be because we really weren't made for going it alone. On more than one occasion Jesus sent His followers out two by two. The apostle Paul, undoubtedly one of the most eminently qualified Christians in history, almost always worked with a team. He was very selective regarding his co-laborers. Certain qualities were required of those who traveled with Paul. John Mark fell short; consequently Paul and Barnabas split up over Paul's refusal to keep Mark on the team (Acts 15:36-41).

COMBINING RESOURCES

There are several very important reasons for teaming up. To begin with, none of us has all the gifts. Alone, we have a limited range of abilities and limited time. Stop for a minute and take stock of yourself. What are your strengths? What are you able to do? How much time do you have in your week for involvement in the lives of other people? What are your limitations, your fears?

If you are like the rest of us, your answers to these questions may discourage you. You may be tempted to give up on having a significant ministry of evangelism before you ever get started, never even getting beyond the stage of wishful thinking. But you probably also know enough about the Scriptures to realize that to be uninvolved is not an acceptable option. Passages like Ephesians 4:11-16 make it clear that there are no bleachers for those who would rather just sit and watch. God's people are to be prepared for "works of service." The Body will grow only "as each part does its work." Every Christian is to be a laborer, involved on whatever level of gifts and maturity he finds himself as he helps to win the lost and build up the saved. So in either direction there is tension! Upon assessing our personal resources, most of us on that first glance conclude that we don't have the necessary equipment to take the message into our own worlds. But staying on the sidelines is also not acceptable. How do we resolve this dilemma?

Among the most basic truths concerning the Church is the fact that it is a Body, an organism. This means God never intended for individual members to function in isolation from one another. True, we are individually accountable to God, but the Christian life and ministry is not to be individualistic. We can't do it by ourselves.

I find it interesting that God has refrained from giving all His gifts to a single individual. Of course He could have done so. At first glance it might appear that He would get a lot more work done today if He would simply give each individual all he needs to carry on a ministry by himself. But instead God has made us all specialists. He has given us gifts in some areas and withheld them in others. We need our limitations as much as we need our strengths. Without our limitations, we could go it alone. With them, we become interdependent. Our limitations serve as the cement that binds us to one another. The end result is greater strength.

So we need to team up. Once you have prayerfully chosen one or more kindred spirits, the next steps are (1) to commit yourselves to co-laboring and (2) to take stock of your assets, putting them to work. This little team of two or more persons will serve as your vehicle for evangelism.

A COMMITMENT TO CO-LABORING

Most of us have three enemies to conquer before we can be free to become truly involved with people. These enemies are busy-ness, inertia, and procrastination.

Busy-ness tends to creep up on us. We begin to participate in an activity in one situation, we accept a responsibility in another, and before we know it every night of the week is committed. We never really intended to let it happen, but suddenly we find ourselves under the tyranny of an endless cycle of commitments.

At this point the second enemy, inertia, moves in on us. *Inertia* is the force that maintains, or gives continuation to, the status quo. We are too busy. We know it. We complain about it. We even know way down in our hearts that we're occupying our lives with the wrong things. But, nonetheless, our lives go on unaltered week after week, year after year. It is hard to break out of our stagnation.

Procrastination is the third enemy. We realize that we are being carried along by a cycle of activities that have a momentum of their own. We know that we are exhausting our lives on matters of secondary importance. We know that the real purposes God has in mind for us are being neglected. We know that we must stop, reevaluate, and regain control over our lives, but we don't. We keep putting it off. We procrastinate.

Jesus said, "Enter through the narrow gate" (Matthew 7:13-14). He was probably referring to a person's choice between salvation and judgment here. But we can take counsel from this analogy of the two gates throughout our lives. Select the narrow gate. Make the harder choice. Don't let life carry you along. "For wide is the gate and broad is the road that leads to destruction, and many enter through it." Following God involves a lifetime of choosing the narrow gates. Paul points out that some of us are going to appear before God like survivors of a hotel fire—with nothing to show for our lives but the pajamas on our backs because we dedicated our lives to perishable pursuits (1 Corinthians 3:15).

Most of us need help to defeat the enemies of busy-ness, inertia, and procrastination.

One of the great life-revolutionizing benefits of becoming accountable to a few kindred spirits is the ensuing restructuring of priorities and commitments. "As iron sharpens iron, so one man sharpens another" (Proverbs 27:17). People who are working together as a team need to allot time to pray together, to open up their lives with one another, and to unite their hearts together on the basis of God's commands and promises. This is the commitment of co-laboring.

OVERCOMING FEARS AND DISCOURAGEMENT

Another benefit gained from teaming up with others is the support it provides for overcoming the fears that always seem to accompany our efforts in evangelism. Often fear is the true cause of our procrastination, at least that has been my experience.

It is strange how fear sets in. To this day I often experience fear when I get into the gospel message with an individual for the first time. Often I'll feel anxiety all day long as I anticipate the conversation scheduled for the evening.

But we fearful souls are in good company. Earlier we observed that Paul also "came . . . in weakness and fear, and with much trembling" (1 Corinthians 2:3). The only personal prayer request he left with his brothers in Ephesus was that he would be able to overcome his fears (Ephesians 6:19-20). The first recorded prayer of the early Church was for boldness (Acts 4:29).

What are these strange fears that perturb us? In some cases there is good cause to fear physical harm. Paul knew all about flogging, stoning, and imprisonment. Believers in much of today's world live under threat of physical harm because of their faith. But remove the physical dangers, and the fears still remain! What do we fear? Rejection? Failure? Embarrassment? Probably all of these.

We might as well make peace with the fact that our fears will always be with us. About all we can do about them is to confess them to one another, and then together to take them to God. Fear in itself is not sin. But when I let my *fears* influence my *actions,* I am acting in unbelief (Mark 4:40). I suspect that this matter of fear was one of the primary reasons Jesus sent the Twelve out two by two. The person who is alone with his fears is the one who will be overcome by them.

"Two are better than one, because they have a good

return for their work: If one falls down, his friend can help him up. But pity the man who falls and has no one to help him up!" (Ecclesiastes 4:9-10).

Inevitably you are going to experience some failures. You will make plans, you will pray over them, you will set out to do what you planned—and nothing will happen. Then what? A very normal response would be to give up the whole idea of having an outreach. Failure is always discouraging. Any new effort is an experiment, and inherent in experiments is the probability of failure. At such times it will take the objectivity of the person or persons you have teamed up with to regroup and keep moving.

TAKE STOCK OF YOUR ASSETS
AND PUT THEM TO WORK.

A few years ago we moved our family to a new city in central Brazil. My responsibilities required that I travel close to half the time, so we chose the city primarily for its schools for the children and because of its airport. Once we were settled, I began to think about a personal ministry. The fact that I spent most of my time traveling, teaching, evangelizing, and helping others in their ministries did not satisfy my personal needs for ongoing involvement with nonChristians and spiritual babes. Of course, my wife and family shared these same needs.

The next eighteen months were sheer frustration. I would manage to make a few acquaintances and then get them interested in sitting down over the Bible with us. Inevitably at that point my schedule would require a four-to-five-week trip. When I would return home, those acquaintances would have all but forgotten my name, and I'd have to start over. This pattern occurred again and again until I was totally frustrated. I thought, "Maybe it's just not possible for someone with a travel schedule like mine to do what I'm attempting to do." But I knew that if I were helping a business executive who had to travel, I would not let him get by with such an excuse.

As my wife and I prayed over this situation, it occurred to us that my ministry team was my own family, and that our ministry would have to begin from within the family's sphere of relationships. Who were our children playing with? Did we know their parents? So my wife and I began to pray for the parents of our children's friends. A friendship began to grow with one couple in particular. We did them favors and they returned them. Since both the husband and wife were professional people who traveled quite a bit themselves, we felt they would understand our situation.

One day my wife and I simply explained our intentions to them. We told them that we were accustomed to studying the Bible with our friends, that we needed this interaction because we wanted to orient our lives around biblical principles. We told them of our frustration because of my schedule. Then I said, "Marge and I have talked it over and we would like to invite you to join us in studying the Bible." They felt honored and we began immediately.

When my next trip took me away, my wife and family were there to sustain the relationships. When I returned, we resumed our studies. This went on for eighteen months, until both the husband and wife understood the grace of God and were growing in Christ. Our team had doubled.

After reevaluating our assets, we decided it was time to reach out again. So we invited two more nonChristian couples to join us. We went back to John 1 and started all over again. But this was familiar ground for the first couple, so in my absences the husband led the discussions. My travel schedule had begun to work in our favor. It was forcing others to assume leadership.

Such were the beginnings of the outreach in which I am currently involved. This outreach continues to grow dynamically to the degree that every participant, even if he has not yet come to faith, does his part. Some participate with hospitality. Others maintain communications among the participants. Others constantly sow among their network of relationships, stirring up new interest. Still others are strongly involved in prayer. Two or three teach. Others keep things organized and moving.

It is important in a group to utilize whatever abilities are found in the group members. If people do what they can do today, tomorrow they will be doing what they couldn't do yesterday.

We could visualize this basic idea with the following diagram:

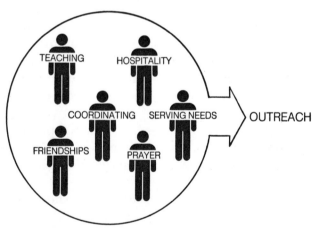

A ministry such as this will constantly have to think in terms of dividing if it is to remain dynamic. This creates a healthy demand for new leadership and increased participation by everybody. Divisions should respect the lines of affinity within the group.

WHAT WILL MY CHURCH SAY?

Very likely a question is growing in your mind as you read this. You may be thinking, "Won't this put me in conflict with my other commitments? What about my church? Won't I be in conflict with the vision and programs of my local church?"

The answer depends on how your particular fellowship defines itself. If your organized church can envision itself as a base of operations out of which the living church (that is the people) operates, then its vision will be broad. If, on the other hand, it envisions itself as a fortress that sends out occasional patrols to gather a few more into its security, then its vision will be narrow. In such cases there could well be tension over a conflict of purposes.

If we, the Church of this generation, hope to touch the lost of this generation, our vision must be sufficiently broad. We must include involvement in the kind of outreach I have just described as an integral and essential part of the Church. Perhaps we need a new definition of the Church, one that draws a large enough circle to include its calling to go into the neighborhoods and the marketplace. But that is a subject for another occasion.

All that is really needed for now is support from your church, permitting you to restructure your priorities and granting you the freedom to adapt your lifestyle to accommodate your ministry.

There are signs of such beginnings. There are churches that are moving in this direction. I heard Gene Getz tell his congregation that one visit to the church building in a week is enough. More than that would rob them of prime time with their nonChristian friends. The rest of their activities should take place in homes.

Joe Aldrich says, "We need men and women that are being urged to go out and mix it up at the front lines . . . with the non-Christian community." He also talks about "deploying Christians into the world."[1]

The kind of evangelistic approach we're talking about can hardly be organized as one more facet of the church program. How do we organize the casual and unstructured hours required for meaningful relationships with nonChristians? This is the Church fulfilling its mission. It is the Church (the Body of Christians) where it belongs—in the world. If we are going to engage the people of this generation, it will only happen on their turf. They will not come to us.

NOTES

1. Joseph Aldrich, from a lecture, "Developing Vision for Disciplemaking."

6

Lighting Up the Darkness

We are the first account of the gospel most people will ever read. Either they will desire more, having read us, or they will decide that there is nothing there for them.

The first two chapters of this book describe the nature of the shifting spiritual climate in parts of the Western world and the effects of this shift on the individual. We concluded Chapter 2 with two questions: What does it take to awaken interest, to induce a person to go back and seriously examine the Christian message after he has already discarded it as an unimportant relic? What ray of hope could penetrate the accumulated layers of disenchantment?

In Chapter 3, we examined how Jesus related to the

people of His generation. We saw how He consistently communicated a single theme: His identity. That man, who for a very short period in human history walked the streets among us, was also God the Creator. As such, He reilluminated a world that had suffered a power failure, where the lights had gone out. He said, "I am the light of the world. Whoever follows me will never walk in darkness, but will have the light of life" (John 8:12). People who believe in Jesus do not spend their lives in the dark. On the contrary, they are able to see where they are going.

Jesus passed the torch to His spiritual offspring. He said, "You are the light of the world. . . . Let your light shine before men" (Matthew 5:14,16). This statement places a very large responsibility on us. He moved on; we stepped in. Just as His manner of life and His speech illuminated the way out of darkness into a relationship with His Father, so we, by our manner of life and our speech, are to bridge this same distance for those who continue in darkness.

"You were once darkness, but now you are the light in the Lord" (Ephesians 5:8). Light catches the eye. Advertisers vie with one another for attention by creatively illuminating their slogans. The reflection from a single mirror in a forest will be seen immediately. If we are light, we will be noticed.

FAITH, HOPE, AND LOVE

What is it that makes the Christian stand out? Unfortunately some of us stand out for all the wrong reasons. Other Christians manage to pass through life virtually unnoticed. But some really do stand out for the right reasons.

Once I participated in a conference in Africa with people from several black African countries. Among them was a young man who had lost his eldest brother a few months earlier. The brother had been witnessing to some Muslim friends, and then one day he was found strangled in his room. The slain brother was the eldest of eight children. The father had died, so he had assumed the headship of the family. The grief and sense of loss was obviously still very strong in the brother who was attending the conference.

There is a significant percentage of Muslims in many of the black African countries. For this reason, Fouad Accad, a Lebanese Christian who has devoted most of his life to understanding Muslim thought, was invited to present a series of lectures at the conference. One does not have to be around this man for long to perceive that he has a singular obsession and love: the one billion Muslims in the world. He exudes love for the Muslim. To hear him talk, Muslims are the most wonderful people on earth.

As Fouad Accad delivered his lectures, the young African who had just lost his brother struggled with what was being said, thinking, "It is easy for those who have never suffered to talk." Fouad Accad, recognizing the struggle, recounted some of his own losses. He told of how the Muslims had sacked his home, carrying off his wife's trousseau and a lifetime of accumulated memories. He told of how his two most faithful protégés had been murdered. These accounts helped not only the young African—they served as a message to all of us. Fouad Accad lives life on a different value system. Because he does, he is able to love those he would otherwise hate. This is what it means to be light.

In everyday terms the difference between the Christian and the nonChristian lies in the fact that the two operate on different value systems. Paul wrote, "These three remain: faith, hope and love" (1 Corinthians 13:13). These three qualities are the foundation stones of the Christian's value system. To the degree that our lives are, in fact, constructed on these three foundations, we are light.

You may be thinking, "This is not exactly the story of *my*

life! Where and how does one acquire this faith, hope, and love?" Interestingly, all three have their origins in a single source: Jesus Christ.

Faith—The New Testament states again and again that the foundation of our faith is in the *person*, Jesus Christ. "Let us fix our eyes on Jesus, the author and perfecter of our faith" (Hebrews 12:2). We "live by faith in the Son of God" (Galatians 2:20). Our faith is based on the conviction that Jesus is what He said He was, and that He will keep His promises.

Hope—Our hope is rooted in three facts about Jesus Christ. First, there is the fact that *He was resurrected* from the dead. "[God] has given us new birth into a living hope through the resurrection of Jesus Christ from the dead" (1 Peter 1:3). Second, there is the fact that *He ascended* to the Father where He constantly defends our case. "We who have fled to take hold of the hope offered to us may be greatly encouraged. We have this hope as an anchor for the soul, firm and secure. It enters the inner sanctuary . . . where Jesus, who went before us, has entered on our behalf" (Hebrews 6:18-20). Third, there is the hope that *He will return.* "We wait for the blessed hope—the glorious appearing of our great God and Savior, Jesus Christ" (Titus 2:13).

Love—"This is how we know what love is: Jesus Christ laid down his life for us" (1 John 3:16). "This is love: not that we loved God, but that he loved us and sent his Son as an atoning sacrifice" (1 John 4:10). Hence, Christian love has the death of Jesus Christ as its source.

Certainly all of us feel woefully weak in these areas of faith, hope, and love. How to grow is the question. The most practical advice I can think of is to suggest you make it a lifetime daily habit to contemplate the significance of what God has done for us in Jesus Christ. Anyone who is truly gripped by these great truths will become transformed by them (2 Corinthians 3:18).

The outworking of faith, hope, and love is very distinct. Each will produce its own fruit in your life. For example, faith will produce both freedom (Romans 14:2) and obedience (Romans 1:5). Love will make you a servant (Galatians 5:13) and will give you patience (Ephesians 4:2).

Hope, too, will bear its fruit. Apparently hope causes the most readily observable changes in a person. According to Ephesians 2:12, the fundamental difference between the Christian and the nonChristian is this factor of hope: "You were . . . without hope and without God in the world." Peter advised people, "Always be prepared to give an answer to everyone who asks you to give the reason for the *hope* that you have" (1 Peter 3:15).

Hope is showy. It produces joy and peace (Romans 15:13), purity (1 John 3:2-3), self-control (Titus 2:11-13), and endurance (1 Thessalonians 1:3). We could go on expanding this list.

Stop and think: What is everybody looking for? Ask anyone. People say they want happiness, peace, freedom, a clear conscience, stability, security. But everything they want out of life is to be found in the hope that comes from Christ. The Christian who appears on the scene with even a minimum of these qualities *will* stand out as a light in the darkness (Ephesians 5:8).

So people are attracted by our *hope*. As they come in closer for a better look, our *love* disarms them, removing the would-be barriers and judgments. Bearing all things, believing all things, and enduring all things, it makes a bonafide relationship possible. In this context, as we explain our hope and exercise our love from Christ, people are led into *faith*.

LIGHT IS MEANT FOR DARK PLACES.

"Become blameless and pure, children of God ... in a crooked and depraved generation, in which you shine like stars ... as you hold out the word of life" (Philippians 2:15-16). This theme—that light is meant for dark places—runs throughout the entire Bible.

But the idea that Christians are to be actively involved in the world creates tension for many of us. Apparently this has been the case throughout the history of the Church. The pendulum has swung back and forth between isolation and compromise from the start. On the one extreme there were the mystics, who isolated themselves from the rest of humanity. On the other extreme we have the example of the syncretistic missionary work that followed on the heels of the conquistadors in Latin America.

This is a tension not easily resolved, caused by the fact that God calls on the Church to exercise two seemingly incompatible functions simultaneously: the edification of the saved and the discipling of the unreconciled. How to do both?!

Once we have a nucleus of Christians, the temptation is almost irresistible to take them off to some safe corner to edify them. The problem is that when we do this, we remove people so far from their peers that further outreach among them is virtually impossible. The edification of the saved must be carried on in the midst of the world, with all its hazards.

This process of isolation I've just described is so common today that few Christians have meaningful relationships with nonbelievers. It has been observed that the average Christian has no nonChristian friends after he's been a believer for two years. Our contact with the world is limited to casual acquaintances. We need to relearn how to build relationships with people outside our normal circle of relationships.

MOVING OUT OF ISOLATION

The development of a friendship tends to follow a predictable pattern. For a friendship to develop between two individuals, one usually starts it off by taking an initiative. He makes some attempt to communicate with the other person. If this overture is accepted, rapport begins to be established between the two. This rapport is reinforced by acts of friendship. Friendship is the context in which good relationships are built.

Let's take a closer look at these four stages of building friendship, listing some possible aspects of each phase.

1. *Taking the Initiative:*
   - Being the first to say hello.
   - Being friendly.
   - Making small talk.
   - Remembering the other person's name and using it often.
   - Being genuinely interested in him.
2. *Establishing Rapport:* Rapport is an attitude of mutual acceptance.
   - Thinking in your heart, "I accept you as you are."
   - Listening with interest to what the other person says.
   - Expressing approval; giving compliments where they are due.
   - Being sensitive to specific needs and opportunities where you could serve.
   - Looking for an occasion to invite the other person to join you in some activity.
3. *Being a Friend:* Friendship has a price tag: time. It means putting people first.
   - Listening; being attentive to thoughts and feelings.
   - Affirming the other person; expressing what you like about him.

- Being transparent; openly expressing your own feelings.
- Allowing your friend to serve you and also to do you favors.
- Accepting him as he is, without trying to reform him.
4. *Building a Relationship:*
    - Letting the other person know what you're thinking, allowing him to see inside.
    - Seeking his counsel.
    - Sharing your personal resources: money, abilities, etc.
    - Making time for him.
    - Not overdoing it; not trying to control him or be possessive.

By no means do I want to suggest that the above list is a prerequisite to evangelizing someone. Evangelism can occur at any point and is often effective in the very early stages. As we proceed through the following chapters we will see how this works out in practice.

BOWLS AND LIGHTS

People do not "light a lamp and put it under a bowl" (Matthew 5:15). With this statement Jesus warns us of the very real possibility of our obscuring the work He has done in us, thereby frustrating the purposes He intends to accomplish through us.

Probably the first thought that comes to mind when we talk about blotting out the light is the factor of sin. "If we claim to have fellowship with [God] yet walk in the darkness, we lie" (1 John 1:6). It is certainly true that a Christian who continues to walk in sin is not giving off much light. But there are several even more subtle ways of burying your light under a bowl. These can easily happen without our perception.

Our Associations—How am I perceived by those I am seeking to win? Usually when two people meet for the first time, immediately the search is on for both parties. Both are busy searching for the appropriate pigeonhole, the proper classification to identify the other. It's not fair, but we all do it.

"What do you do?" I ask you. (The answer to that one gives me lots of clues. I can now begin to speculate on your social status, your financial situation, and your educational background.)

"Where do you live?" (That's another question equally rich with misleading information. The city or the part of town helps me modify and embellish the image I'm creating.)

"Where did you go to school?"

"What did you study?"

"Oh, do you know James? How did you come to know him?" (Pay dirt! I've identified a mutual acquaintance. And since I already have a pigeonhole for James, my research is nearly completed. After all, people are known by the company they keep. It's not fair, but that's the way it is.)

When we approach people with the gospel, the same procedure occurs. "What church is he from?" they think. "Is he with some sect?" "What is he trying to get me into?"

This factor of identifying someone by association is a very difficult one to deal with. As we discuss the gospel with people, one of the implications is, "If you accept this message, you'll become like me." And if our Christianity is integrally and exclusively identified with a particular denomination, church, or organization, then we will be rejected by others before we know what has happened. The secularized person is just not looking for something to join. He quickly rejects unnecessary identity changes.

A few years ago some friends of mine organized an evangelistic thrust aimed at university students in their country. They worked out an approach, had materials printed, and then proceeded to systematically interview students in their residences. Their objective was to generate interest and participation in some evangelistic Bible studies.

My friends interviewed 800 students, but they were defeated before they began. They just didn't realize it. At the top of the materials they distributed was the heading, "(the name of their organization) Invites You. . . ." They thought they were inviting the students to look at Christ. But the students saw them as people who were inviting them to join their organization. Only three of the 800 showed any response! Organizational appeals and calling programs inviting people to church rarely stir secularized people to a response.

Obviously no Christian would consciously allow his own name or identity to compete with the name and identity of Christ. We would be shocked and chagrined to discover such a turnabout. The problem, then, is not with how we view ourselves but with how we are perceived by others. A good question to constantly ask ourselves is, How am I perceived by those I'm seeking to win?

Our Expectations—This second "bowl" under which we sometimes hide our light is related to the first. An exaggerated commitment to our religious identity often goes hand in hand with an equal concern for that group's growth and success. The success of a church is customarily measured in terms of people. Numbers of people participating at various levels in church programs are studied and reported as a part of our process of evaluation. Because of this focus on church growth and programs, the temptation becomes almost irresistible, as we reach out to the nonChristian, to approach him with his entire agenda already worked out ahead of time. We scarcely consider whether or not he is ready for what we have for him—or whether or not that will truly fit him.

Our expectation is that new Christians will like what we have for them and that they will conform. We expect them to fit into our structures, respond to our forms, participate in our activities, and embrace our patterns of conduct. It is unbelievable how quickly a person who is considering Christ will pick up on all this. Sometimes he accepts the new patterns and fits in. But more often he reacts negatively. I can look back on my own ministry and give you the names of people I alienated with this kind of manipulation. They just disappeared. They never explained why, but in retrospect it is obvious what went wrong.

Thus we can eclipse the light by our expectations. When we mix our own desires for personal or corporate success into our evangelism, we compromise its true purpose.

Our Expressions—One common characteristic of every subgroup is that each has its own terminology. I live in Brazil, where it takes only a few minutes of conversation on spiritual issues to identify a Catholic from a Protestant, and one kind of Protestant from another kind of Protestant, on the basis of the choice of words alone. There is no problem with this, as long as each sub-group person is among his own kind. But our primary interest is precisely to go to those who are not of our own kind. I've seen our use of religious terminology put people off again and again. Consequently it, too, can be another "bowl" that obstructs the light.

As our Bible study group was just beginning to expand among our neighbors, several nonChristians who had no Christian background began to participate. Most of the participants worked together in the same hospital, so soon the word about our Bible study began to get around.

One day one of the participants told me he had a colleague who was interested in attending. I agreed that it would be good to invite him. So Marcos showed up at our next study. He turned out to be a beautiful, mature Christian man. No wonder his Bible was tattered—he seemed to know it by heart.

But as I led the group in our discussion, I quickly realized I was in trouble. As soon as I would ask a question, before anyone else had time to think, Marcos would give the answer. Now I wasn't looking for answers to my questions. I already had those. I was trying to get the group to think. To complicate matters even further, his answers were always right—unintelligible to the rest of the group, but right. They left nothing else to be said.

So I tried another tactic. I asked a question and then gave a cross-reference passage where the answer could be found. That didn't work either. Before the others discovered whether the passage was located in the Old or New Testament, Marcos had found it, read it, and commented on it—all of it, of course, in the Portuguese equivalent of King James. The recourse for me was to lapse into lecturing, which is the least effective means of communication in these kinds of situations.

One evening, at the end of a study, one of the wives commented to me, "I know I can't say things the way Marcos does, but I need the chance to express myself, even if what I say isn't very profound. But just when I open my mouth, Marcos has already said it." I knew she was right. The next day I invited Marcos over to my home. I explained the situation and we agreed it would be better for him not to continue with us. That was a difficult day for me.

Any biblical term that is not a part of our everyday language needs translation. Some of these are very common words for us: grace, sin, faith, justification, reconciliation, regeneration, walking in the Spirit, etc. Technical theological terms are also confusing. When we talk about dispensations, ecclesiology, or eschatology, we will certainly mystify many people. Then there are the in-house terms. An individual is referred to as "brother" or "sister." We talk about "receiving Christ," "going to the throne of grace," and so on.

Our prayers, too, have certain patterns. Many Christians seem to have a special voice, with certain intonations they reserve for religious occasions.

We need to try to hear ourselves with the ears of those we are seeking to reach.

Our Actions—We often obscure the gospel by our scruples. For some unfortunate reason, we Christians are generally known for what we abstain from. If our reputation was one of abstaining from immorality, injustice, and dishonesty, it would be wonderful. But the list is not that noble. It consists primarily of how Christians are to behave, especially in areas where the Bible does not give specific instructions. We impose these norms for behavior even though the Scriptures specifically instruct us to refrain from passing laws on doubtful issues. Colossians 2:20-21 says, "Since you died with Christ to the basic principles of this world, why . . . do you submit to its rules: 'Do not handle! Do not taste! Do not touch!'?"

Three years ago, a young couple came to Christ while spending a few months in Mexico. Soon afterward, they returned to their home country. We didn't have much hope that they would grow spiritually because they were so new and because they would probably be cut off from further help. But when they arrived in their home city, they immediately began to teach the little they knew to their friends. Soon there was a nucleus of seven couples looking to these new Christians for help in their spiritual growth.

Being nominally Roman Catholic, the couple turned to the local priest for help. That didn't work out, so they located a Protestant missionary. After a few months of involvement with this missionary, the couple became alarmed at the effects. At great personal expense, they returned to the person who had first helped them understand the gospel and asked *him* to promise to bring help to them. Their explanation was, "We did not step out of one set of traditions just to enter another. What we need is someone who will teach us the Bible only."

This young couple precisely identified the problems that our norms of Christian conduct create. These norms introduce a second authority into our Christian fellowship: tradition. The effect of these contrived external norms presents a false concept of what the Christian life really consists of. This in turn puts off those who would otherwise be responsive.

A TREASURE IN JARS OF CLAY

Our associations, expectations, expressions, and actions all add up to the image we project. This matter of image *is* important because ". . . we have this treasure [the gospel] in jars of clay" (2 Corinthians 4:7). The first response of the nonChristian will be related to what he sees in us. In affirmation evangelism, the message is inextricably linked with the messenger. So each of us needs to ask, "When a nonChristian looks at me, who does he see? Is my lifestyle attractive to him?"

As you can see, this kind of evangelism can hardly be called an activity in which one engages on certain occasions. It is *life*. Living itself becomes evangelistic. We draw nonChristians into our lives and step into theirs. As the relationships expand, so does the gospel. As Joe Aldrich puts it, "Evangelism is a way of living beautifully and then opening up those webs of relationship to the nonChristian."[1]

NOTES
1. Joseph Aldrich, from a lecture, "Developing Vision for Disciplemaking."

7

Taking the First Steps Toward Christ

During a recent visit to my hometown, I conducted a short workshop on evangelism. An old friend of mine was in the audience. Twenty-five years earlier he and I had spent many hours together. Because he was a new Christian then, I had tried to pass on to him the things I had been learning about discipleship.

During that initial time together, I showed him how to explain the gospel to another person. Then he and I did some evangelism together. Next I had him make up a list of his friends and business associates. After he showed me the list, we prayed together over those names for several weeks. Then I encouraged my friend to invite his acquaintances out for lunch, one at a time, to share the gospel with them.

After the workshop, this friend came up to me and said, "You sure have changed." "Yes," I replied. "I have." He reminded me of the process I had taken him through twenty-five years earlier and of how he had presented the gospel to each of his friends. "I did that," he told me, "until all my friends were gone!"

I had thought I was teaching my friend to evangelize. But in reality I was contributing to his isolation from the very people he most wanted to win for Christ. I had made the mistake of encouraging him to attempt to reap among people who had not yet been prepared.

PRESENTATIONS POLARIZE

For years I lived with a very simplistic understanding of evangelism. I viewed it as a matter of being alert to opportunities to present the gospel to a friend or acquaintance so that he could make an intelligent decision about whether or not he was going to open his life to God. Where the opportunity didn't naturally present itself, I would proceed to create one.

Dewey Johnson and I were classmates. His manner convinced me that if he weren't already a Christian, a simple conversation would take care of it. So I began to watch for a chance to talk to him. But as the weeks passed, I realized no natural opportunity would ever come along. So I invited him to go fishing with me.

Afterwards, as we sat and cleaned our fish, I began to talk to Dewey about the gospel. I had never been more mistaken about a person in my life. Dewey Johnson was far from being a Christian, and, what's more, he didn't even want to talk about the subject. My attempt so polarized our relationship that further communication became impossible. Things were awkward between us from then on.

If I had only known then some of the things I've learned since then, it probably would have been a different story with Dewey. In *Evangelism as a Lifestyle,* I developed the thesis that evangelism is a process that includes planting and cultivating as well as reaping. When we ignore this truth, when we persist in our attempts to reap where the soil is not prepared and the seed has not borne its fruit, polarization rather than conversion is frequently the result. The reason for this is obvious. Implicit in the gospel presentation is a call to make a decision. An insistent or an insensitive evangelist will inevitably force the nonChristian who is not ready to submit to Christ to back off, to create some distance between himself and those who are attempting to evangelize him.

SUCCESS STORIES TO THE CONTRARY

As you read this chapter, you are probably thinking about the people you know or have heard of who tell of how they put their faith in Christ the first time they heard the gospel, with no previous sowing or preparation. Perhaps it even happened that way with you. I am sure there are those exceptions, but it would hardly be wise to spend our lives in the pursuit of the exceptions. Also, a closer examination of an exception often reveals that it was, in fact, not an exception at all.

In reality, the sudden conversions we find in the New Testament came about as the result of considerable preparation. The Ethiopian eunuch was returning from a religious pilgrimage and was reading the book of Isaiah when he first heard the gospel (Acts 8:26-39). The first Roman convert, Cornelius, was described as a devout, God-fearing man who gave to the poor and prayed to God regularly (Acts 10:1-2). The apostle Paul had, as his form of preparation, the heritage of sixteen centuries of biblical content and a powerful vision that struck him down and left him blind (Acts 9:1-9). In Philippi, where there was no synagogue, God prepared an instant harvest via an earthquake that would have cost a jailer his life had it not been for the apostle Paul (Acts 16:25-34).

It is so true that we are "God's fellow workers" (1 Corinthians 3:9). Where God has already made the preparations, we can and should proceed to reap. But very often what God has in mind for us to do as His fellow workers is to *prepare* the harvest. "Thus the saying 'One sows and another reaps' is true" (John 4:37).

The question then is not which one is right, proclamation or affirmation. Both have their place. Rather we need to ask, *Which* do we use *when?*

Dawson Trotman, founder of The Navigators, used to pray that God would use him in the life of every person he met. That is a good request to pick up on. If coming to Christ is a process, why not help every person we meet to move just one step closer to Christ? Some people are only a step away and it would be our joy to assist in the birth. Others are farther out, but that doesn't mean the step we help them take would be any less significant.

Basically our social relationships are of two kinds. There are the chance encounters with strangers, and there are the more permanent relationships with friends, neighbors, and colleagues. The passenger in the next seat is an example of the first. The neighbor who asks you to sign his petition is an example of the second kind. When we think of sharing our faith, it is important to keep this distinction in mind, even though our immediate objective is the same—to help people take the next step.

In the case of a casual encounter, we need to exercise discernment to determine a person's background and thinking. We should be prepared to explain the gospel, but should avoid doing injustice to the person by forcing a premature presentation, by pressing the issue unduly, or by being over-bearing. In most casual encounters, our witness will be supplemented by the reinforcement of other influences God is bringing to bear. On occasion we will be able to leave a person with a clear understanding of the essential message. When we are led to do this, we can be assured that God will use that witness in a positive way.

In the case of our more permanent relationships, we must be acutely sensitive to the attitudes and emotions of others. The gospel is urgent news, but that doesn't mean we have to rush and push to get it across. According to 2 Peter 3:9, God is holding up the judgment of the world and the ushering in of His new creation until the stragglers cross the threshold. We can therefore assume that if God uses us to start something in someone's life, He also intends to bring it to fruition. Therefore, we need to evangelize the people in our daily world by reinforcing the relationships between us in the process rather than by polarizing them.

Most of us have only one sphere of friends and acquaintances. We can either see this sphere transformed into an increasingly fertile environment for the gospel, or we can quickly exhaust it with a slash-and-burn approach. The intent of what I have defined as *affirmation evangelism* is to make the most of the opportunities our more permanent relationships offer us.

MINI-DECISIONS

I commonly hear people express a desire to know how to break into discussing the gospel with an acquaintance. As one put it, "I need to develop a positive, nonthreatening introductory statement, something that gets me into the subject with someone. What do you suggest?"

Usually what people are looking for is a one-step launch

question—something that will carry them gracefully from a dead stop into an effective discussion about Christ in a single motion. In situations where God has already prepared the way it's hard to go wrong at this point. Almost anything you say will do. Philip simply asked the Ethiopian man if he understood what he was reading. Peter asked Cornelius why he had sent for him. But most of the people we meet are neither reading the book of Isaiah nor have they had any recent visions. For the unprepared, there is no one easy step from where they are to where we want to go with them. This question of how to launch into the gospel in one step is equivalent to asking, How do I set the ball for a seventy-yard field-goal attempt?

Rather than looking for a single step, it is better to think in terms of *mini-decisions.* If evangelism is a process, then our function is to accompany our acquaintances down the road to Christ, showing them the way. We must walk the road with them, a step at a time. So we think in terms of steps, or mini-decisions. We can diagram the process as follows:

DISTANCE FROM CHRIST   CONVERSION

When we see things from this perspective, our question changes. Rather than asking how to present the gospel in such a way that this person who is a long way out will respond, we begin to ask what needs to happen if this person is to be drawn to Christ.

We evaluate the resources at our disposal: God has made us light; we have the Holy Spirit; and we can pray. This is a formidable arsenal. Then we proceed, counting on God to effectively work in the situation as we use these resources.

The first steps toward Christ can begin with seemingly insignificant things: initiating a hello; doing small favors; borrowing and loaning things among neighbors; conversing over the fence. These grow into larger acts of friendship and hospitality such as a night out together, picnicking, etc.

As the distances are reduced, observe closely. Try to understand the needs and interests of your new friends. Don't try to build your witness on the problem side of their lives or you'll get off on the wrong foot.

Eventually you will begin to elicit from your friends some of the following "pre-conversion decisions" about you:

- He's okay.
- I'd like to get to know him better.
- I feel comfortable with him. He accepts me.
- I'm going to find out why he's so different.
- It seems that he gets his outlook on things from the Bible.
- He's a Christian, but he's okay.
- Being a Christian sure has its advantages.
- I like his friends. I envy their confidence.
- It might be interesting to look at the Bible someday.

Now our diagram looks like this:

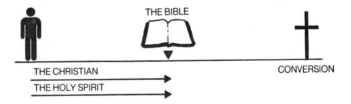

When a nonChristian comes to the point where he is responsive to the idea of seeing what the Bible has to say, many of the major hurdles to faith have been overcome. The path that remains between his unbelieving state and faith in Christ becomes relatively smooth. This is because *the spiritual arsenal is now complete.* The Holy Spirit can now take up the sword that "penetrates . . . dividing soul and spirit . . . [and] judges the thoughts and attitudes of the heart" (Hebrews 4:12). For this reason it is far more effective to first aim toward bringing the nonChristian to the point where he wants to examine the Bible with us. To have this as our first objective rather than thinking in terms of a single explanation of the gospel at an opportune moment offers some very large advantages.

If handled properly, our examination of the Scriptures together with the nonChristian *reinforces* rather than polarizing the relationship. Also, it allows us to lay a foundation of truth that will serve as a basis for faith. It gives the individual the time and freedom to fight and win the battle against his defiant will that has been saying no to God ever since physical birth. In short, the spiritual birth will be a healthy one.

So we add the following factors to our diagram:

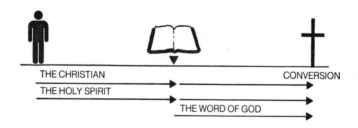

. . . AND MORE MINI-DECISIONS

Once the nonChristian has begun to examine the Bible with us, we can expect a new series of mini-decisions to occur. We might expect him to say, for example:

- The Bible isn't impossible to understand after all!
- The Bible says some important things.
- What the Bible says about life fits my experience.
- Jesus seems to be the key. I wonder who He really was.
- Jesus is God.
- I need to do what He says.

Central to successful evangelism among people in the main-stream is getting them to examine the Bible with us in a context of affirmation and acceptance. This is in contrast to the more common approach where we count on a single presentation to move a person from unbelief to faith. But what we are suggesting is probably new to many and there-fore gives rise to further questions. Some of these are: How do I get people who don't even believe the Bible to want to study it? How can I keep their interest up so that they will continue week after week? What do I do with all the questions they are bound to ask that I'll never be able to answer? What about reaping? When and how do I do that? We will be addressing these questions in the following chapters.

8

Bridging the Distance from Indifference to Faith

The world's least attentive audience would probably be found on the Friday afternoon flights between La Guardia Airport in New York and National Airport in Washington, D.C. These flights are always full of businessmen, many of whom make that same trip a hundred times a year. Invariably before takeoff the stewardess comes on with the routine safety instructions. As she goes through her explanation, the inattention is absolute. She is endured, and everyone is relieved when she has finally finished.

She fails to hold the attention of her audience for two reasons. In the first place, nothing she says is news. Everyone aboard has already been through it countless times. In the second place, the dangers for which she is preparing the passengers are very remote. The felt need for what she has to say is just about zero.

What would it take for her to capture the attention of her passengers so that they would actually listen and finally learn how to use one of those oxygen masks? Suppose the plane developed serious mechanical problems at 20,000 feet and began to lose altitude. If that same stewardess would then repeat those same instructions to those same passengers under those emergency conditions, she would have everyone's total attention! People are motivated to learn to the degree that the subject matter is perceived as relevant to needs or wants.

The secularized person has quit listening to the voices of religion for similar reasons. He has concluded that no news (new information) will ever be forthcoming. The Christian claims and warnings appear hopelessly redundant. If we are to recapture his attention, we must begin at the level of his felt needs and aspirations.

That is why Jesus said what He did to Nicodemus. Nicodemus had climbed as far as he was going to in the Jewish hierarchy. His achievements were his security. So when Jesus said, "You'll never make it unless you undergo a second birth," He had Nicodemus's attention. To a woman in the midst of her daily chore of hauling water, Jesus began talking about water. To a fisherman He talked about fishing. To the hungry He talked about bread. He began with the familiar, the daily concerns, and from these mundane matters He transported His listeners into new dimensions of understanding.

Apathy is the most difficult obstacle we can face. Apathetic people just don't care. They are indifferent. They are like the roadway in Jesus' parable of the sower (Matthew 13:4), which was so hard that when the seed was sown it bounced and then just lay there until the birds finally found it and devoured it. Hardness is not belligerence or toughness; it is indifference. She can be a sweet, fragile, 115-pound teen-ager—and still be spiritually hard!

Some people give the impression that they are indifferent about everything. They have seen it all and disbelieve it all. But that is only an impression. Everyone cares about something, and that something is our starting point. We can be confident that whatever the starting point, the ultimate word on it will be God's Word. So our objective is to begin with a person's felt needs and then lead him to the point where he sees that those desires of his, whatever they may be, are ultimately met in Christ.

STARTING POINTS

One obvious implication of what I've just said is that there is no single approach, no skeleton key that will unerringly unlock people's interest. Often we will need to forge new keys to fit particular situations. This is not unusually difficult. We must begin by being observant and sensitive. Here are a few examples.

1. *Young parents*—For many Brazilians the family is still high on the priority list. If you ask a graduating university student in Brazil about his aspirations, he will frequently tell you he is looking forward to marriage and children. He wants a comfortable family life, and wants to be able to provide well for his wife and children. The Brazilian society is child-oriented. It is also basically Freudian.

At graduation the individual is often virtually impervious to the gospel. He is engrossed in other things. He is bent on getting into his profession, getting married, etc. But if we look in on this young family six or seven years later, we will find that life is not going exactly as planned. The family is feeling the consequences of their Freudianism. Mom and dad are now living under the dictatorial regime of their three-year-old, who has just stepped up his reign of terror to combat the recent intrusion of the newly-born sibling.

The parents are at a loss. Afraid of damaging their child's psyche by disciplining him for his behavior, they elect to endure the pandemonium. But it's too much. They begin to take their frustrations out on one another, and soon the last vestiges of the earlier aspirations are dead.

Now, at last, there is a felt need!

We have picked up on this need by putting together a series of discussions on how to raise children according to the Bible. We find that parents are at such a loss that even though they have ignored the Bible all their lives, they are eager to see what it has to say about child rearing. Although the Bible and Freud are in disagreement on almost every point, and although these parents would not be ready to recognize the Bible's inspiration, the Bible consistently ends up as the undisputed authority in our discussions. The experience of all parents tells them that what the Bible says is truth.

In this way, instruction in child rearing serves as an almost irresistible bridge from indifference to keen interest for young parents.

2. *University students*—Had we started out with these same Freudian individuals ten years earlier, they would have been totally indifferent to receiving instructions on child rearing. As students just beginning their university studies, their needs and interests would have lain elsewhere.

The first years of university life offer the long awaited opportunity to get out from under the scrutiny of parents, brothers, aunts, and uncles. There's room to think, to question, to act. If there are any philosophical inclinations in a person, they will come to the surface at this stage in life. The student will look for some way to explain his existence and to justify his own behavior. So we have a different starting point.

In this case our bridge out of indifference might be along the lines of the following sequence of statements.

a. Man exists. Either he is here by chance, having evolved, or he is here by Creation. If there is a Creator, He has to be intelligent and powerful. The question is, which of these alternatives is true? (Figure 1)

FIGURE 1

b. The equipment we have at our disposal to research the answer to this question is our five senses. Everything we know has been received through hearing, seeing, tasting, touching, and smelling. (Figure 2)

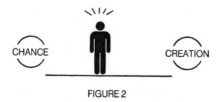

FIGURE 2

c. If there is a God, and if He is Spirit, He would be beyond the range of these senses. He would go unperceived. Science, which researches only by extending the reach of those same senses, will never provide answers on God.

d. Therefore God would be unknowable—unless He somehow took the initiative to reveal Himself to man.

e. The basic claim of the Bible is that God *did* make Himself knowable by entering our time and space world. (Figure 3)

FIGURE 3

f. Jesus of Nazareth claimed to be that revelation. Either He was who He said He was, or God remains unknowable. History records no other serious claimant to Deity. (Figure 4)

FIGURE 4

g. This simplifies our search, reducing it to a single question: Who is Jesus? If He is who He said He was, we have answers to life. If we conclude that He isn't who He claimed to be, we also have our answer. In that case our answer would be that there are no answers.

Based on the possibility of this claim being true—that God could be seen, touched, and listened to in Jesus (1 John 1:1-2)—we have a basis for inviting the nonChristian to investigate the question, Who is Jesus?

3. *The post-Christian*—The above sequence is effective among people who are asking the existential questions. But among many of this generation, such questions are as good as dead. The secularized Europeans we described in Chapter 1 would be an example of people who have given up on the big issues. They readily admit that they have no answers, but they are also quite convinced that no one else has any either. So, they reason, why bother to search? It's better to busy the mind with whatever happens to catch your attention.

To those of us who have been raised in the Aristotelian tradition of linear logic, these people are baffling—incomprehensible! But they are no exception to the rule. They, too, have needs and desires that can serve as bridges to Christ as effectively as any other. It's just that the bridge has to be quite different. It may not be built along a sequence of ideas at all.

For the secular European and his American cousin, relationships are of primary concern. There is a certain irony in this because although they place relationships at the top of their value system, they are, at the same time, unusually inept in this area. In part their weakness is due to the fact that they were raised on bad relationships. Sensing that their spiritual inheritance went bankrupt before it ever got to them, they realize that the only thing that remains that can possibly give cohesion to life is other people. So the needs and desires in this area of relationships—love, affirmation, and acceptance—serve as ample footing for building their bridge to Christ.

The Bible has a lot to say about relationships, and discussions on the subject can be attractive and helpful. But in the case of this bridge, the practice is far more effective than the theory. Talking about love and acceptance is no substitute for the real thing. Simply move into a meaningful relationship. I've seen many people of this generation led into the Bible and on to Christ for no other reason than that they had been unconditionally befriended by the evangelist. The invitation to examine the Scriptures was accepted, not as a result of any overwhelming arguments or strong feelings of a need for answers, but simply because it represented one more opportunity to enjoy the love and warmth of that relationship. Logic, I'm convinced, is overrated as a persuader. It finishes a poor second to love every time.

These three illustrations of bridge building are intended to be just that: illustrations. Hopefully they will inspire some creative thinking on how to build bridges to fit the needs and aspirations of those you are seeking to win. There are many others, such as the pursuit of success, having a successful marriage, etc. Before going further, we should stop to ask ourselves two questions: (1) What are some of the felt needs and aspirations of the people I am desiring to reach? and (2) In what way could these needs and aspirations serve as bridges?

The next logical question, which we will address in the next chapter, is, How do we go about getting our friends onto these bridges, moving along toward Christ?

9
Going to the Primary Source

There are primary sources and there are secondary sources. A primary source is an eyewitness. In the sciences, he is the person who does the experiments. He does basic research and surfaces new information. Secondary sources report on things that primary sources have seen and done.

Reliability is a problem with information of any kind, especially with any information that comes from secondary sources because they are never totally free from personal biases and subjectivity. Communicators do not have to intentionally lie to be misleading. As a person's own subjective perceptions are mixed with the facts he is reporting, distortions just happen.

The news media serve as an excellent example of how variable communication can be. Even if everything reported on a given issue is true, the simple act of choosing what to include and exclude, or the amount of time and space given to an issue, can determine favorable or unfavorable public sentiment.

Another example of variable communication is the broad range of history books. A quick comparison of a Mexican history book with an American history book, where the same events are recounted, reveals that frequently the heroes and the villains have changed hats. Bravery is alternately described as brutality, and an insignificant episode is interpreted as a great victory, depending on which country published the book.

When it comes to communicating the gospel to the secularized person, we strengthen our appeal immeasurably by letting him know we intend to confine ourselves to an examination of the sole primary source that we Christians claim: the Bible. Although the average secularized person does not accept the inspiration or authority of the Bible, the idea of taking a look for himself at this famous book is likely to be very attractive to him. It defines the parameters of the discussion for him, and for us. He thus feels that the odds are more even, that he will be free to think and decide for himself.

Frequently the nonChristian fears being indoctrinated and manipulated. Christian books and tracts abound; they are in endless supply. Although many of them can be extremely helpful, all of them fall into the category of secondary sources. They are someone's perception of the primary source. As such, they are often viewed with suspicion by the nonChristian. He is never sure he is really getting the full story. Thus the skeptical or wary nonChristian who keeps his distance will often respond favorably to an opportunity to do some original investigation—*if* the environment is right. So our goal is to create that right environment as we simultaneously lead the nonChristian to see the wisdom of taking time to personally research a subject of this magnitude.

GETTING USED TO THE IDEA

Most people automatically reject new ideas. Since it's part of human nature to resist change, whenever it's forced on us we react. This is because change is usually accompanied by a sense of loss. The familiar gives way to the unknown. Someone has described change as occurring in four stages: rejection, tolerance, acceptance, and assimilation. The first time we're confronted with something new, we tend to reject it. But after it is around for a while, we become tolerant of it. Then we begin to see its positive possibilities; we begin to accept it. From there it's a small step to assimilating the idea; we make it our own.

When a nonChristian is first introduced to the idea of examining the Bible, he will often reject it. So we introduce the idea without calling for a response. "Someday I'd like to show you how to read and understand the Bible on your own." Or, "Someday I'm going to invite you to our Monday night Bible study." "Someday" is vague, noncommittal. But by reading a person's reaction to such a statement, it is not hard to gauge whether that day should be arranged for the next week or the next month—or postponed until further notice.

After you repeat an abstract invitation of this sort several times, two things often begin to happen. First, your nonChristian friend has time to become accustomed and increasingly receptive to the idea. Second, he's beginning to wonder when you're going to get around to making your invitation good. The shoe is suddenly on the other foot. He's looking to you to keep your promise.

GETTING STARTED

Our immediate objective is to help a person begin to examine the Bible. From there on, our purpose is to lead him into an understanding of its central message: that Jesus is God and that one passes from death to life through faith in Him. This purpose can be summarized in two questions: (1) Who is Jesus? (2) What does He want of me?

The strategic importance of these two questions can easily be missed in the midst of the 66 scriptural books with all their diversity. As we invite a person to begin to examine the Bible on his own, we need to help him simplify his research task down to these essentials. The dialogue may go something like this:

A: If you're interested in examining the Bible, I'd like to help you get started.

B: I'd like to see what it says, but I think you need to know that I don't believe it the way you do.

A: That's fair enough. It's the only primary source we Christians have. If, after examining that source, you decide that it is not true, you have your answers. You can lay to rest your questions about God and go your own way. If, on the other hand, you find truth in the Bible, then you also have *your answers.* Either way you win.

B: That's fair enough.

A: Now, the Bible is different from other books. You don't just pick it up and read it from cover to cover. The Bible consists of 1,189 chapters, divided into 66 books. It was written by many different authors over a period of roughly 1,600 years. To sit down and read it through in order to research your questions would be the equivalent of going to a library with a question and reading your way randomly through the books on the shelves to get your answers. It would be better to get some help from the librarian. He can save you much time and frustration by helping you pull the right books off the shelf. That's what I'd like to propose to you: that I be your librarian.

B: I'd like that.

A: Okay, let's set a time.

We pick up the dialogue at the agreed upon time and place. It's in a neutral, familiar spot, either in your house or in his. You have brought along an extra Bible, one with page numberings that are identical to yours. You are using a modern translation, intentionally avoiding the paraphrased versions. Explaining that the particular rendering of the passage isn't in accord with the original intent doesn't exactly build credibility in the Bible. Nor does it help to have to explain that "quit you like men" simply means "be courageous."

A: The Bible is divided into two parts: the Old Testament and the New Testament. The Old Testament has to do with things that went on before the time of Jesus Christ. The New Testament starts out with four eyewitness accounts of Jesus' life. Then there's a book that records the first years of the Christian movement. The remainder of the New Testament consists of letters written to the fledgling groups of Christians, or churches, that had begun to scatter out around the world in that first century A.D.

   The theme of the whole Bible, the Old and the New Testaments, is the same. It is that God is revealing Himself to man with the intent of rescuing him from his self-destructive rebellion. The basic claim of the Bible is that the man Jesus of Nazareth is the apex of that revelation.

   The Old Testament was written to get the world ready for this revelation. The New was written to record the event and to explain its significance.

B: I follow what you're saying, but I can't promise I'll arrive at the same conclusions you have.

A: Of course not. All I'm asking is that you take a look. Whether the Bible is truth or not is beside the point. For now, the important thing is for you to understand that the Christian position stands or falls on this one figure, Jesus. If He does not prove to be what the Bible claims for Him, then Christianity offers no answers for anyone. Can you see that?

B: I see your point.

A: My proposition is to give you the opportunity to examine the Bible for yourself so that you can draw your own conclusions on this question of Jesus' identity.

B: Right!

A: As I said before, the New Testament begins with four books that we call Gospels. They are four eyewitness accounts of the life and teachings of Jesus. Why four? It is as if four people standing on separate corners of an intersection witnessed an accident. The four testimonies, although essentially the same, will vary according to where they were positioned and what details especially caught their attention. By combining four testimonies, any event would be more thoroughly recorded. This is the effect of the four Gospels. The sum of the four gives a quadraphonic record of Jesus' life.

I'd like to propose that we begin with the fourth Gospel, the Gospel of John. John was one of Jesus' closest friends, so what we have in this book is an eyewitness account by someone who knew Him intimately. His account begins on page 1,137. Let's begin by reading the first three verses.

B: "In the beginning was the Word, and the Word was with God, and the Word was God. He was with God in the beginning. Through him all things were made; without him nothing was made that has been made."

A: Did you understand that?

B: No.

A: I don't blame you. Let's see if we can decipher the meaning. What does the word "Word" refer to in this passage?

B: I don't know.

A: Look at verse 14.

B: "The Word became flesh and lived for a while among us."

A: So evidently this "Word" became a human being. Who would that be?

B: Jesus?

A: Right. Now reread the three verses putting Jesus in place of the word "Word." What is John claiming about Jesus?

B: That He existed in the beginning. That He was God. That He created the world. But I can't agree with that!

A: I'm not asking you to agree, remember? My part is just to help you understand what is written here. Would you agree that this is what John is claiming about Jesus?

B: Yes, but I can't accept it.

A: Fine, let's go on. Could you read the next two verses?

And so it goes. Our purpose is to guide our nonChristian friend through the book of John, helping him understand what the book says concerning two questions: (1) Who is Jesus? (2) What does He want of me?

Our immediate concern is not to extract agreement or to win arguments; it is to produce understanding. We need to leave room for disagreement and doubt. It is the *Holy Spirit* alone who convicts of sin, righteousness, and judgment, not us. It is the *Bible* that reveals the true intents of the heart. We should leave these responsibilities where they belong. Our part as we co-labor with God is to bring the nonChristian into contact with these powers, and to love him as he struggles his way out of his rebellion and into faith.

A set of guideline questions for the book of John has been included as the Appendix at the back of this book. They are not comprehensive, and with experience you will undoubtedly come up with additional questions that will serve better than mine. But I offer them as a start. It's usually best to try to cover one chapter of John at a time. Obviously, you'll not exhaust the contents of a chapter in an hour's discussion. But if you can't resist going into every little detail, you'll soon be studying by yourself again!

Now back to our dialogue. An hour or so has gone by, and we have just finished the first fourteen verses of the first chapter of John. We refer back to our original invitation: that we would help our friend research the message of the Bible for himself. At this point, as far as he knows, this is the first and last discussion the two of us will ever have on this subject.

> A: That's enough to get you started. My impression is that you are getting ahold of the meaning of the text. How do you feel about it?
>
> B: It's complicated, but, yes, I'm getting it.
>
> A: It gets easier from here on as John begins now to narrate events in Jesus' life. Do you want to continue?
>
> B: Yes.
>
> A: Let's pick it up from here next time. In the meantime, if you feel like reading ahead, do it. Underline anything that strikes you as being especially interesting or significant, and put a question mark in the margin beside anything you don't understand. Let's get together again in a week or so and discuss your observations and questions.

KEEPING IT GOING

Rather than asking for a commitment to study through the entire book of John or even for a six-week commitment, it is better to take it one week at a time. The more loosely we hold people, the freer they will feel around us. If we establish expectations, and then if they don't fulfill them, there will be a sense of failure. We can avoid this simply by not expressing expectations or by not setting any standards. The continuing of the studies must depend on genuine interest in the subject and on the strength of the rapport or friendship between the two of us.

The importance of reaffirming our relationship in between the Bible sessions cannot be overstated! A fifteen-minute drop-in visit or even a quick phone conversation communicates acceptance and interest on our part. Leisure time together is better yet. When you're with him, talk about him, about things that are of interest to him—sports or even the weather. *But* don't just talk about the Bible. We will soon wear thin if we are only conversant on the first chapter of John.

Sometimes the nonChristian is totally unabashed among his friends about his awakening interest in the Bible. More often it is the other way around. He struggles with feelings of embarrassment and fears of being ridiculed. We need to be aware of these feelings. Nicodemus came to Jesus at night because he didn't want his colleagues to know of his interest in this controversial man. Jesus, of course, realized this, but he didn't send Nicodemus away to come back when it was daylight. A person on his way to Christ is already battling with his inner demons. He doesn't need any additional enemies at the moment. So we need to be discreet and reassure him.

One way to honor this compunction of our friend is to be careful about where and when we meet to study. The location should be neutral and private. Church buildings are out because they are not neutral. Restaurants and offices are not private enough. Homes are good.

Many years ago a friend and I conducted some evangelistic rap sessions in several fraternities on a particular campus. We got ourselves invited to conduct discussions. In most cases, the fraternity members would gather in the lounge and we would make our presentation, eventually throwing the session open for questions. Afterwards we would organize those who were really interested into study groups.

In one fraternity we decided to have the study in Jack Smith's room. It went great the first week—we thought. But we had taken the rest of the fraternity by surprise. The following week they were ready for us. Apparently they had spent the entire week getting ready for us!

Everything was normal for the first thirty minutes. Then suddenly a mocked up radio program blared from a tape recorder placed just outside the door. There were a few phrases of music. Then came the commercials; more music; then more commercials. The commercials advertised such things as Genuine John-the-Baptist Road Sandals and Pictures of Jesus that Glow in the Dark. Jack Smith and the other fraternity brothers participating in the study were mortified. My feelings were more of frustration. Our study was being interrupted! As I look back on this episode, I can hardly believe we did what we did next. We continued to meet in Jack Smith's room! The other brothers fled the study, so it was only Jack and us. What could he do? We were using his room! The harassment continued. Finally when Jack's social life was in ruins, he got up the courage to tell us he never wanted to see us again.

Somehow we justified what we did in the name of boldness. But the pressures that accompany being identified with Christ always come soon enough. We should be the last to contribute to them!

In this chapter we have treated the subject of getting started on a one-on-one basis. Very often this is where it all begins—

with one individual. If we start out with the idea that before anything can happen we must organize a group of nonChristians, we could easily overlook the individual opportunities. Frequently these prove to be the greatest in the long run! But the approach we have described here can, of course, also be applied effectively on the small-group level.

10
Guiding Someone Through the Scriptures

A good question is the best possible teaching tool. Because Jesus was the foremost Teacher, no one could ask questions the way He could. Frequently with a single question He penetrated to the core of even the most controversial issues.

> "Which is easier: to say . . . 'Your sins are forgiven,' or to say, 'Get up, take your mat and walk'?" (Mark 2:9)

> "Show me a denarius. Whose portrait and inscription are on it?" (Luke 20:24)

> "But what about you? . . . Who do you say I am?" (Matthew 16:15)

"John's baptism—was it from heaven, or from men?" (Mark 11:30)

Jesus' questions made an impact. They drew from His listeners conclusions they would never have faced up to otherwise. A study of the Gospels for the purpose of observing Jesus' use of questions and their effect on others is a course in communication in itself.

Communication takes place whenever understanding is transferred from one person to another. It is not what we manage to *say* to someone that is important; it is what is *heard*, what sinks in, that matters. The use of questions is especially effective in communication because this harmonizes with the way our natural thought processes work. As we think, we constantly pose questions to ourselves: What do I need to do next? When can I work that in? At what percentage point does the other option become favorable?

The sciences are structured on hypotheses and research. A hypothesis is a statement that serves as a question. Research either confirms, disproves, or modifies the hypothesis. As we repeat this testing process, we make progress in our understanding.

I have entitled this chapter "Guiding Someone Through the Scriptures." "Guiding" is more descriptive of what we should do in the course of evangelizing than either "telling" or "teaching." Our purpose is to guide the nonChristian into the Scriptures in search of truth. We must recognize that his basic assumptions and values are not Christian. Some reconstruction must go on at this primal level of assumptions before he comes to faith, and this reconstruction takes time. It involves discoveries and reformulations on his part. Much of this will be subliminal, but it will take place. We need to be patient guides during this process.

If we limit our understanding of evangelism to telling

(declaring the propositions of the gospel) or to teaching (giving instructions regarding the body of truth), we will not have the staying power needed to work with people who must make a full 180 degree turn in their personal presuppositions and values. Such people need room to think in a stimulating, accepting environment. Learning to ask the right kinds of questions is key to meeting these needs.

Generally we don't give much thought to asking questions. We're usually more concerned about being able to *answer* the questions nonChristians customarily pose. In fact, Christians often fall prey to two misconceptions. They are the two sides of a single coin, which go like this:

- I'm not qualified to get involved in evangelism because I can't seem to answer people's questions.
- I'm ready for anybody because I've learned the answers to the ten top questions nonChristians ask.

The ability to ask questions is every bit as important as the ability to answer questions. We'll see why as we move along in this chapter considering *how to ask and how to answer questions.*

HOW TO ASK QUESTIONS

We are prepared to lead a Bible study only when we have formulated a few questions that will draw the other person into discovering the relevant truths of a passage. The ability to do this presupposes, of course, a fair understanding on our part of what the passage says and means. That will take some work, especially the first time around.

In Chapter Five, we talked about the importance of making evangelism a team effort. We will need that team at this point because few of us have the initiative or discipline to persevere week after week in Bible study when left to ourselves. Hence, one of the first activities you might do together could be to study the book of John, or whatever book you choose, chapter by chapter. You would study with two purposes: to understand the text for yourself and to formulate questions to use with others.

Questions can have three functions. They can (1) launch a discussion on a subject, (2) guide a discussion, and (3) serve to summarize what has been said. The following are examples of launch, guide, and summary questions:

Launch: What observations did Nicodemus make about Jesus in verse two?

Guide: How did Jesus respond to these observations?

Summarize: What can we conclude from this dialogue about our human abilities to understand spiritual matters?

The questions on the book of John in the Appendix are mostly launch questions. You will find that as you actually get into the discussion of a passage you will be able to improvise most of the guide and summary questions. It is helpful to bear in mind that questions can serve all three of these functions. It is possible, with a proper use of questions, to move the discussion into deeper levels of communication.

There are a number of rather standard *guide* questions that are frequently useful. Some of these are:

- Why do you think he said that?
- What do you think he was getting at?
- What else do you see in this verse?
- Why do you say that?
- What do you mean?
- Why do you think he uses the word "_____" here?

There are also some basic *summary* questions that you could use:

- How would you summarize the main idea of this paragraph?

- How would you say this in your own words?
- How would you summarize the idea we've been discussing?

We have described three *functions* that questions can have in a discussion. There is also a variety in *kinds* of questions. There are questions for:

- *Understanding:* What does it say? What else?
- *Interpretation* or *Clarification:* What does this mean?
- *Justification:* How did you arrive at this conclusion?
- *Direction:* Mike, what do you think?
- *Comparison:* Where did we see this same idea before?
- *Application:* How does this affect us?

A WORD OF CAUTION

We began this chapter by saying that questions are the best possible teaching tools. But they can also be used as weapons. In careless hands they can kill or maim communication in a minute. This is because questions are seldom neutral. A question is also a statement. The statement behind the old question "When did you quit beating your wife?" is obvious. But there is also a statement behind an apparently innocuous question such as "How does this chapter apply to you?" With one or two similar questions we can checkmate the person we're studying with at any time. It might go like this:

- What does this chapter say about you? (This chapter talks about you!)
- Would you agree that what it says is true? (You must change!)
- What do you think you should do about it? (You must change now!)

With a few well-placed questions of this sort, what started out as an accepting environment with time and room to think was transformed into a verbal war game. And we have just ended it by pinning our quarry to the wall. It's so easy to do, but it will happen only once.

The wise thing to do is to restrict our application questions to those of a more general nature, such as "Did you learn anything about yourself in this chapter?" Then stop; back off. Give the other person the room he needs to make his 180 degree turnabout. He'll get there.

HOW TO ANSWER QUESTIONS

When a nonChristian begins to study the Bible with you, one of his biggest unspoken questions will be, "To what degree will I be able to express what I really think with him? What will be the reaction if I express my true doubts and questions?" The person will first send out some rather "safe" trial questions. How we react to these questions will affect the level of communication between us from then on. If we respond with dogmatism (which is a form of insecurity) or with defensiveness (which is another form of insecurity), the nonChristian will quickly understand the rules of the game and will proceed accordingly. He will either operate within our limitations—or he will disappear. But if we demonstrate an attitude that encourages the expression of doubts and questions, our effectiveness will be far greater.

QUESTIONS ARE WELCOME.

Even more effective than *asking* a good question is *being asked* a good question by the person you are guiding. When the discussion of a passage is conducted on the basis of the questions the other person raises, the relevance of the discussion increases. So we should give the nonChristian the first chance. After reading a paragraph, we first ask him what questions come to his attention. Sometimes he doesn't really understand enough to ask a question, but often he comes up with enough to carry the discussion. If, after he has had his opportunity, an important truth remains unaddressed, we can come in with our own questions.

When we approach our guiding session in this way, we create a climate where all questions—even questions unrelated to the text—are free to flourish. These are the questions the nonChristian has carried for years but has never had the freedom or opportunity to raise before. It is important to give these questions a genuine welcome when they come up. They may scare you to death when you don't have a notion of how to answer them, but you can worry about that later. The important thing is to receive the nonChristian's questions positively.

THREE KINDS OF QUESTIONS

Why do people ask questions? The motive is not always a desire to learn. They may not even want an answer. Sometimes questions are asked with the intent to trap or embarrass. We'll call these *captious questions.* Or a person can ask a question in an effort to escape, to justify his own actions, or just to buy time. We'll call these *self-defense questions.* Then there are straightforward questions that are truly motivated by a desire to know and learn. These are *honest questions.*

Questions need to be answered according to their intent. As the writer of the Proverbs artfully put it, "Do not answer a fool according to his folly, or you will be like him yourself. Answer a fool according to his folly, or he will be wise in his own eyes" (Proverbs 26:4-5). In other words, if we miss the intent or fail to perceive the motivation behind a question, we will fall into the other's trap. To try to give an honest answer to a captious question is to play the fool.

There are many illustrations of these three kinds of

questions in the dialogues recorded in the Gospels. It is instructive to observe the way Jesus responded to questions. Rather than taking a question at face value, He responded according to the motives of the questioner. In a dialogue in Luke 10:25-37 we have examples of how Jesus handled both a captious question and a question asked in self-defense.

"On one occasion an expert in the law stood up to test Jesus. 'Teacher,' he asked, 'what must I do to inherit eternal life?' [A captious question. Rather than seizing this "opportunity," notice what Jesus does with it.] 'What is written in the Law?' he [Jesus] replied. [Rather than answering, He countered with a question. Jesus essentially asked him, "How do you read it?"]

"He [the expert in the law] answered: '"Love the Lord your God" . . . and, "Love your neighbor as yourself."'

"'You have answered correctly,' Jesus replied. 'Do this and you will live.' [People who ask captious questions are not looking for information, so Jesus gave this person none. He only reminded him of what he already knew. But that was enough to put the aggressor on the defensive.]

"But he wanted to justify himself, so he asked Jesus, 'And who is my neighbor?'" [A self-defense question.]

Jesus typically replied with a story, the parable of the Good Samaritan, which He typically concluded with another question: "Which of these three do you think was a neighbor to the man who fell into the hands of robbers?"

"The expert in the law replied, 'The one who had mercy on him.'" Self-defense questions are frequently very much like this one, in which the legalist attempted to split hairs over who constitutes a neighbor. Such questions are raised in an effort to evade personal responsibility or to justify oneself. Jesus' final reply, "Go and do likewise," certainly did nothing to restore the man's equilibrium. He probably felt devastated as he came away from that exchange.

But Jesus had all the time in the world for those who came with honest questions. "When he was alone with his own disciples, he explained everything" (Mark 4:34).

Jesus is an impossible act to follow. But we can take some lessons from Him. We can either weary ourselves in vain preparing and expounding our irrefutable arguments and apologetics in response to insincere questions, or we can separate out the questions that come our way, taking the serious questions seriously and not allowing the others to disturb us. We need to realize that even if we could satisfactorily answer the captious questions, it would make little difference in bringing the questioner closer to Christ! So our responses need to be in accord with the *intent* behind the questions.

UNDERSTANDING THE INTENT OF A QUESTION

If we are successful in creating an affirmative environment for the nonChristian, he should feel the freedom to raise all sorts of questions. He may test you with probing questions before asking *honest* questions. Often the intent of a test question is not malicious as in the case from Luke 10. Rather, the questioner wants to see if it will be safe for him to ask his more serious questions. It serves as a trial balloon. It is not easy, nor is it necessary, to identify the intent of every question. But there are a few simple guidelines that, if followed, can help sort out the questions for us.

WHAT DIFFERENCE WILL IT MAKE?

When the nonChristian asks a question, you need to ask *yourself,* not him, several questions: "What difference will it make if I answer this question? What will he do if I give him a satisfactory answer? Will he accept it and build on it? Or is this question more of a general statement of rejection than anything else?"

If, after asking yourself these questions, you conclude that the nonChristian's question deserves an immediate answer, and if you feel you are prepared to answer it, go ahead and deal with it.

One characteristic of the honest question is that the questioner is willing to wait for his answer. It won't bother him if you say, "That's a good question but I don't know how to answer it at the moment. Let me study it this week and I'll show you what I find out the next time we get together." The person who is trying to test or trap you, however, will want his answer on the spot. But we've already seen how, when the motives are not right, our best answers won't make any difference anyway.

WRITE THE QUESTIONS DOWN.

Questions that arise out of the text you are studying are usually honest questions, which should be treated as they come up. But since nobody has all the answers, inevitably some questions will arise that we won't know how to answer. That won't bother the other person if it doesn't bother us. To say "I don't know, but I'll try to find out" will build credibility rather than undermining it as we might fear. We should write such questions down, and then come back with the answers when we have them.

Questions that are unrelated to the text, that come out of the blue, are the ones that require closer scrutiny. For example, what if someone suddenly asks, "If Jesus is the only way, what will God do to the heathen who have never even heard His name?"

There might be one of several motives behind such a question. It could be asked in a captious manner, in which case the question is not really a question at all. It is simply a statement trying to justify the person's unbelief by saying that God is not just.

Or, the question could be asked in self-defense. Perhaps the discussion is getting too close to home for comfort. The person needs time and space. He senses either you or the Holy Spirit closing in on him, and he's not ready for that. So he throws in a difficult question to halt the advance. Sometimes the person really does need that space, and you should allow him to have it. If the intent is similar to that of the legalist's question, "Who is my neighbor?" we should not give an answer.

It's not difficult to avoid being caught in a diversionary tactic of this sort. You can say, "Now that's an important question and we'll get to it. Let me write it down." Have the person repeat it so you can record it. By writing a question down, you communicate that you are taking the other person seriously, listening to him and respecting his concerns and doubts.

The next time you meet, you need to be sure you have that piece of paper with you. As you begin the session, take it out and place it on the table before you. This will communicate a great deal. It will say, "I've not forgotten your question. We'll get to it, and if you have any similar questions, they are welcome too!"

QUESTIONS HAVE A SEQUENCE.

Frequently it is impossible to answer a particular question for the simple reason that it has been asked out of sequence. For example, how can we discuss the justice of a God whose existence is in doubt? We can no more answer questions out of their sequence than we can put a roof on a house that hasn't yet had its walls framed up.

This idea, that questions have their sequence, should be communicated to the person with whom we are studying. This helps him understand why we are postponing answering some of his questions, and it makes him feel free to add new questions to his list.

By recording extraneous questions as they come along rather than attempting to answer them immediately, we are able to retain control of the direction of the dialogue. We can decide when and how to deal with these questions. Thus we can neutralize the wrong motives present when a question is first raised. The desire to trap or test us fades as we consistently demonstrate love and acceptance. As the relationship grows, the nature of the questions will change.

There are important exceptions, of course, to this idea of responding to questions according to their sequence. Frequently it becomes apparent that a particular question is, in fact, blocking the road to progress toward Christ. Even though we may not have had the time yet to lay the foundations for an answer, we may realize that the questioner really needs some kind of an answer before he can go on.

On such occasions our response could go something like this: "I can see this is an important question to you, so I'll try to show you what the Bible says in answer to it. I wouldn't be surprised if the answer doesn't satisfy you [he has not yet conceded to the authority of the Scriptures], but just for your information, this is what the Bible says about this question."

Whether the person accepts or rejects the answer we give in this situation is secondary. The important thing is to answer the question from the Bible.

STICK TO THE BIBLE.

When studying with people who don't believe the Bible, it is especially important to consistently use nothing but the Bible.

Our position is: "You're not ready to accept the authority of the Bible? That's understandable. One of the reasons we're sitting here together is to give you the opportunity to judge for yourself whether the Bible speaks the truth or not. So I'll try to keep my own opinions out of the discussion. We'll consider my personal opinions to be no better than anyone else's. When you ask a question, I'll try to restrict myself to showing you what the Bible says in response."

Any other position eventually serves to undermine the authority of the Bible. Once we mix opinions, whether our own or those from secondary sources or traditions, with truths from the Bible, we create a second authority: man himself! Whenever this occurs, man eventually ends up having the last word.

This attitude of letting the Bible speak for itself must be based on our own deep confidence in the Bible. Since it is the truth, it is authority. As such it is fully capable of taking care of itself. As it addresses the issues of life and as it speaks of man and his society, it always rings true. As this occurs again and again, the nonChristian, usually subconsciously, simply begins to concede to the Bible's authority. Rarely do I even discuss the authority or inspiration of the Scriptures with a nonChristian. Sometimes people are curious about how the Bible came into existence. A brief explanation of its historic origins [which can be found in a volume such as *Halley's Bible Handbook*] is usually sufficient.

THE WATERSHED QUESTION

There is one key question that, when answered, unlocks the answers to most of the other questions. Many of the previously impossible questions become easy, if not redundant. This watershed question is, of course, the one we raised in Chapter 3, that of Jesus' identity.

Jesus' identity is the premise upon which our other answers are constructed. For example, until a person acknowledges the deity of Christ, he is faced with an unresolvable dilemma when it comes to his relationship with God. This dilemma is described in Luke 7:29-30: "The people . . . acknowledged that God's way was right, because they had been baptized by John. But the Pharisees and experts in the law rejected God's purpose for themselves, because they had not been baptized by John."

One group said God was just; the other said He wasn't. Those who said He was just had been baptized by John; those who said He wasn't just hadn't been baptized by John. But what did John's baptism have to do with a person's position on God's justice? It was a baptism of repentance. To repent means to conclude that you are in the wrong. We have to come to that conclusion before we can admit that God is right.

In other words, if God is just, I am not just. But if I am right, then God is wrong. Since I'm not ready to admit I am wrong, God has to be the one who is wrong. Therefore I find some injustice in Him. This is where the questions about the destiny of the heathen, the Indian, or the severely retarded child frequently have their origin. It is the reason why man, after he himself has transformed this world into a hell, blames God for the mess. Either we must find something wrong with God, or we must assume the blame ourselves. But if we assume the blame, we also sentence ourselves to judgment with our own words.

When we settle the question of Jesus' identity we can bring ourselves to face up to our own injustice. It would be quite valid to translate Romans 1:17, "In the gospel the *justice* of God is revealed."

You question God's justice? Examine Jesus' life. Was He ever unjust? No. But also, in Him, there is deliverance from our own unjustness. We can face up to it.

Once this is understood, the remaining questions almost answer themselves.

- You have a question about God's existence? That question is redundant now that we've identified Jesus as God.
- What is God like? Look at Jesus.
- What are the origins of the world? What is man? What is life all about? The answers to these and similar questions are found in what Jesus had to say about these things.

SUMMARY SUGGESTIONS

As you grapple with the matter of guiding someone through the Scriptures, here's some practical advice:

Things to do—

- Remember that "telling is not teaching."
- Remember that your job is to guide into the discovery of truth.
- Rely on the Scriptures by letting the Bible assert its own authority and letting the Bible reveal the truth.
- Use questions as your primary teaching tool.
- Learn to handle philosophical questions.
- Learn to capitalize on serious questions.
- Allow the person you are guiding to think and discover the answers.
- Keep conflict between the individual and the truth, not between the individual and you.
- Be aware of and sensitive to feelings and apprehensions.
- Make the individual comfortable.
- Control the characteristics of the study.
- Control the makeup of the group.
- Keep a list of difficult questions, and answer them in their logical sequence.

Things to avoid—
- Avoid arguing in defense of the Bible.
- Avoid debating on any subject.
- Avoid giving the answers, especially dogmatic answers.
- Avoid feeling threatened by the strength of the opposition or by your own lack of knowledge.
- Avoid defending philosophical positions.
- Avoid insisting on agreement.
- Avoid judging behavior.

Results to expect—
- The Bible will assume its authority.
- The Bible will overpower with truth.
- The Holy Spirit will do His part, both revealing and convicting.
- The identity of Christ will become evident.

11

A Time to Sow, A Time to Reap

"As for you, you were dead . . ." (Ephesians 2:1).

Our ministry is to the dead. That's what evangelism is: working among the dead. But death is repulsive. It is ugly. We want to get away from it so we don't have to look at it.

So it is with the spiritually dead. Their behavior is often ugly and embarrassing to us. We feel offended by the things they do and say. We're anxious to get them converted so that they can clean up their act. But the world is not a nice place to live in, and often the people of the world are neither respectable nor nice to be around. Nevertheless, it is precisely to these people that we are sent.

Jesus said, "It is not the healthy who need a doctor, but

the sick. I have not come to call the righteous, but sinners to repentance" (Luke 5:31-32). Later He communicated the same idea in His parable of the wedding banquet. According to this parable, when the upper social set began to make excuses, the king sent out his servants to stand on the street corners to gather in the poor, the crippled, the blind, and the lame. Thus the wedding hall was filled with many social rejects (Luke 14:15-24).

It is so easy to judge others, to measure others by our own criteria for acceptable behavior. But what realistic expectations should we have for people who are spiritually dead, who come to us maimed and blinded? What expectations should we have for the person who was abandoned when he was eleven years old? What about the man who has to overcome his resentment against his religious father who left him to clean up the financial and moral mess when he skipped town with his mistress? Repeatedly in the Old Testament, God says He punishes the children for the sins of the fathers to the third and fourth generations. Anyone who has spent much time around people of the world understands the terrible truth of this sad legacy. There is a law of cause and effect: like father, like son (Exodus 20:5). Aberrant behavior is the norm for those we are sent to win. This decadence has been passed on from parent to child. Thus we should be neither shocked nor offended by what we encounter.

We are so given to judging others. It is so easy to carry judgment and criticism in our heart against the nonChristian. We feel so virtuous when we condemn the husband who abandons his wife and emotionally cripples their children in the process. Instead we should weep. The dead are dead. They are under the spell of "the ruler of the kingdom of the air" (Ephesians 2:2). That is the reality of the situation. We must be cognizant of the distance and the difference between the living and the dead if we are to have the tolerance and patience necessary to accompany someone in his pilgrimage out of the dominion of darkness into the kingdom of God's Son.

For the great majority of people, the road to Christ is long. Although He is near, man is so very far. Belief systems have to be turned around. Many people have to do a total about-face. James Engel summarized the belief system and the presuppositions that commonly prevail among what he calls modern man:

> God, if He exists at all, is just an impersonal moral force.
>   Man basically has the capacity within himself to improve morally and make the right choices.
>   Happiness consists of unlimited material acquisition.
>   There really is no objective basis for right and wrong.
>   The supernatural is just a figment of someone's imagination.
>   If a person lives a "good life," then eternal destiny is assured.
>   The Bible is nothing other than a book written by man.[1]

The contrast between a system of belief such as this one and the Christian position defines the distance that needs to be reckoned with as we take the gospel to this generation. This vast distance is not going to be closed by confrontation, debate, and rebuttal. We do not win people by proving to them that they are wrong. Rather it is the beauty and superiority of Christ that makes them realize there is a better way. But such a realization takes time. My own experience is that frequently the nonChristian will spend a year or more becoming acquainted with Christ through the Scriptures before spiritual birth occurs. But such births after an adequate spiritual gestation period are always healthy. The babe lives.

A TIME TO SOW:
SUSTAINING INTEREST WHILE
PLANTING AND CULTIVATING

How do we sustain interest? How do we keep a person coming back for more, week after week, when he's not even a Christian?

We have already given several answers to this question. It is the love and acceptance. It is the absence of manmade norms and expectations. It is our refraining from using the person for our own personal success. It is the opportunity we offer him to take an honest look at the primary source. It is the steady prodding of the Holy Spirit through the Word of God. These are the basic factors that keep people interested. But there are other lesser, perhaps more technical, things to keep in mind as well.

1. *Watch the tempo of your Bible discussions.* Frequently someone will tell me, "Man, we went until midnight in our discussion last night. They didn't want to quit."

That may be true. Maybe they didn't want to quit. But they are probably sorry today that they didn't as they wearily drag themselves through the day. Next week they'll think twice about whether they have the physical and emotional energy to go through another similar dose. Don't let a discussion drag on. Quit while you're ahead, before people want you to.

Observe this principle as you work through a chapter. Keep moving. Don't try to wring the last drop out of every question. Be the first, not the last, in the group to decide it is time to go on to the next paragraph.

In short, don't bore people.

2. *Keep your content relevant.* When the people you are guiding through the Scriptures comment on how profound you are, it is probably not a compliment. What they are really saying is that they are having a hard time making sense of

what you're talking about. Truth, in its essence, is simple.

Discussions become tedious when we belabor the theoretical or the doctrinal side of things. They become alive when we succeed in correlating what the Bible says with everyday experience.

Content must speak to the hearer. It is not necessarily what catches your attention in a chapter that is important but what is relevant to the hearer. There can be a large difference between your needs and interests and his.

3. *Take no-shows in stride.* Don't take offense when the nonChristian cancels out at the last minute or simply doesn't show up. It is an inevitable part of the dynamic of the process. The nonChristian is ambivalent about the time he's spending in the Bible. He wants to continue, and yet he doesn't! As he begins to understand the implications of the Christian message, this ambivalence frequently evolves into a real inner struggle. This is progress.

One of my friends, as he gives his testimony describing his pilgrimage of several years toward Christ, tells of how he stood me up. He would be on his way over to where we met, looking for the slightest pretext for changing his plans. Often he would simply decide to stop and have a beer with a friend rather than going on.

When this would happen, I'd let a couple of days go by. Then I would drop in on him at the bank where he worked. We'd go have coffee together and spend a few minutes chatting. I would never ask him why he hadn't shown up. (I already had the answer to that.) And he would never offer any explanations. As we'd say goodbye, I'd ask, "How's Thursday night, after the evening news?" So it went.

We should respond to no-shows with acceptance. We get back on track by touching base—in person, if possible. Touching base is important no matter how well things seem to be going. A quick visit or even a phone call confirms the friendship and prepares the way for the time when the struggles begin.

4. *Preserve the affinity in group situations.* Recently a lot of debate has been generated over what is being referred to as "homogeneity." Donald McGavran was the first to expound what he calls the *homogeneous unit principle.* Essentially what he is saying is that people don't like to gather with others who are different in any major way. Therefore, a church will not grow if it is heterogeneous. Those who disagree claim that McGavran's principle is based on pragmatism rather than on the Bible. The Bible, they point out, teaches that all are one in Christ, that there are no real walls of human differences between people. McGavran's defense claims that the other side suffers from idealism.[2]

To talk about the fellowship of Christians is one thing. But to have any expectations along this line for the lost is quite another. We began this chapter by saying that to evangelize is to work among the dead. Christian love can only come from people whom the Holy Spirit has restored to life and made whole. According to the Bible, it is more realistic for us to expect attitudes of resentment and conflict from the nonChristian.

Enigmatically, although it is often this unique oneness among Christians that captivates the nonChristian, he himself is incapable of behaving in the same way. He may be inspired by our comments about God being no respecter of persons and about the Body of Christ being one. He might agree that these ideas are true and right. But they will do nothing to alter his dislike for the new couple we are trying to integrate into the group.

Frequently, simply because of a lack of affinity, the nonChristian will drop out. He'll just disappear without causing a ripple. It's a very relevant fact that we will not successfully sustain interest among people arbitrarily grouped together without due consideration for natural affinity.

5. *Maintain a good group balance.* It should be obvious that an evangelistic Bible study should favor the nonChristian rather than the Christian. But I've frequently seen three or four Christian couples attempt to gang up on a nonChristian couple or two. This is almost always extremely intimidating for the nonChristians. They become self-conscious about their ignorance of the Bible and fearful of asking their real questions. They are afraid that their questions will appear stupid, or that they will be rejected if they reveal their deeper disagreements with the Christian position. Not wanting to be disagreeable, they often simply choose not to verbally disagree. Real communication becomes almost impossible in such a context.

A good study should be informal, casual, and non-threatening. The atmosphere should be one of acceptance—low-key and relaxed. Under these conditions, a lot of strange ideas will be expressed. But that's good. It's essential that freedom of expression exist, that there be room for incomplete and erroneous conclusions. We don't have to set everything straight at once. But where the group is made up predominately of Christians, someone will inevitably be unable to resist. Someone will turn to a chapter and verse to "set the record straight." The nonChristian's interest will not be sustained for very long when the thinking process is consistently stifled in this way. This potential stumbling block leads us to a final suggestion for sustaining interest.

6. *Hymns and prayers are out.* So are sermonettes. It is sometimes difficult for people who have been raised in a church environment to perceive how they come across to the nonChristian. Often they do things automatically without even stopping to question their propriety—things that strike the non-religious person as very strange.

For example, when I open my Bible in private, I have

formed the habit of stopping to pray first, asking God to help me understand it. When I'm finished, I usually find myself praying again, this time asking God to help me make what I just learned a part of my life. But I neither open nor close a study with a nonChristian with prayer. I refrain from this for two reasons. First, the nonChristian is unable to participate in talking to Someone whose existence to him is still in doubt. But more importantly, opening or closing a discussion with prayer is viewed as a religious form by the nonChristian, and that is usually enough to formalize the discussion! It changes the environment.

Pray before and after your discussions, but do it in your heart—to God, not as a subtle sermon to the nonChristian. If you feel like singing, do that the same way. To the non-religious, a hymn and a prayer and a sermon equals a church service. So we should discuss rather than lecture, lead rather than teach, and we should do our singing and praying in our hearts to God.

A TIME TO REAP: DECISION TIME

In *Evangelism as a Lifestyle,* I discussed the fact that three elements of personality are involved in making a decision to become a Christian, or in making any significant decision, for that matter. They are the *emotions,* the *intellect,* and the *will.* The emotions contribute the desire, the intellect provides the reason, and the will commits the person to action. A decision that is made solely on the basis of emotions or merely as a result of intellectual assent—any decision that does not include the commitment of the will—is a non-decision. Such decisions fail the tests of time and pressure. Our stereotype New Year's resolutions illustrate this point.

In making a decision to become a Christian, the involvement of the will is fundamental. This is because it was our will that got us into trouble with God in the first place. Adam's sin was an act of rebellion against God's headship. Conversion is laying down our arms and coming out with our hands up. It is submitting again to God's sovereign rule over one's person. As we saw in Chapter 3, this is the meaning Jesus gave to the word "believe." To present conversion as anything less is to misrepresent the gospel.

Whatever overt response a person makes to express a decision to become a Christian (whether it is a prayer, a testimony, or a request to be baptized), it must be a reflection of an inner transaction with the Holy Spirit. More often than not, as we evangelize people in the way we are describing it, this transition occurs when we're not around. We'll know when it has happened by the changes in the person's attitudes and life. Sometimes the first signal is a sudden change in pronouns. Rather than "you Christians," the person speaks of "we Christians." Or the first indication may be a voluntary testimony.

Although we cannot bring about the inner transformation from death to life, we can do a lot to assist in the process.

As we move along through the Scriptures with a non-Christian, his attitude usually begins to change. In the beginning his questions and responses may reflect unbelief, doubt, or even belligerence. But there will come a time when the rejection is gone. The intent of his questions will change. This means he is proceeding on from the initial question, "Who is Jesus?" to the next question, "What does He want of me?"

When this shift in attitude occurs, it is time to sharpen the focus on the essential message. We need to give the person a summary of the gospel and a clear definition of what he needs to do by way of response. He needs to be made aware of the fact that there is a decision to be made.

Frequently, after a few weeks, as we sit down to study, I

will suggest that rather than going on to the next chapter we should do something different this time. I tell the person that I'd like to show him an illustration summarizing the central message of the Bible. I then proceed to show him the Bridge illustration. This illustration shows how Christ is the bridge over the chasm separating death from life. If we're studying the book of John, I use verses from that book as our basis. I cross-reference the main points with passages in other parts of the Bible in order to clarify what we're saying and to demonstrate the harmony of the Bible. (This illustration is included in the Appendix, page 213.)

My purpose in using this illustration at this point is not to call on a person to make a decision. Rather it is to plant the idea of deciding in his mind. So, when we are finished, instead of asking him, "Where would you place yourself on the diagram?" (he has already mentally done that), or, "Do you see any reason why you shouldn't make the decision now?" (he probably *is* intellectually persuaded), I say, "This illustration summarizes the central message of the Bible. Fold this page up and keep it in your Bible and we'll refer back to it as we go along." From that time on, we use this diagram to summarize our discussions. At the end of each discussion, we take it out and talk about how the contents of the chapter we just covered fits into the overall picture.

Summarizing the gospel in this way has several significant effects:

- It facilitates an understanding of the Bible because it provides a basic framework to which the parts can be related.
- It seeds the inner thought that a decision needs to be made.
- It clarifies what this spiritually ripe person must do by way of response.

As one person with whom I've studied put it, "Every day

when I get up in the morning, I ask myself the simple question, 'Is today the day I'm going to cross that bridge?'" It is helpful for the person who is on his way to Christ to understand what we have said in this section about the place of the emotions, the intellect, and the will in the decision-making process.

Several years ago a friend wrote to me from another country where he was just getting started as a missionary. In his letter he told me that he had been studying the Bible with many nonChristians for several months, but that he was about to give up on them. They had come to the point, he said, where they all understood and accepted the truth of the gospel. But none of them had submitted to Christ. Since they openly admitted they were just not willing to make that decision, he was ready to give up on them and move on. He wanted to know what I thought.

In my reply I congratulated my friend on getting those people to the place where they understood the real issue so clearly. I said that in the final analysis the will is always the issue, and that when a nonChristian can admit this fact we should celebrate rather than become discouraged. That's progress. My friend stuck with that group, and eventually they became the foundational people for his ministry in that country.

It often helps a person when we say, "Just to clarify where we are, my impression is that you have just about satisfied your questions on the intellectual level. The real issue now is whether or not you're going to let God have your life. Would you say this is the case?"

Intellectual questions usually don't survive for long. Even with someone coming out of agnosticism or atheism, the intellectual questions are frequently satisfied in a matter of a few weeks. But the will is a different story. It can hold out indefinitely.

WHEN DO WE GIVE UP?

God will not override a person's will. Man can persist in saying *no* right down to the end. I suspect a person can give God a final *no,* and that God will accept that decision and leave him alone from then on. We need to be sensitive to God's leading on this point.

The whole process we have been describing must be borne along with prayer. We pray our way through every discussion. We look to God in prayer to do whatever is necessary in a person's life to bring him to Christ. God's responses to these prayers are observable. We take our cues from God on how long to persevere with someone, staying in there as long as God does, but no longer. Our cue to desist is when an individual quits fighting and makes peace with his decision to not allow God into his life.

MAKING THE ASSIST

The problem with a premature decision is that it puts words into people's mouths. They think they've done something they in fact have not. It's hard work to act like a Christian when you're really not one. No one can keep it up indefinitely, and eventually a person has to quit.

But procrastinating over a decision is equally dangerous. People who know better often die in their sins. Sometimes people just need a gentle shove. It might go like this:

> A: We've been examining the Bible for six months now. How's it going? Where would you say you are in your progress toward Christ?
> B: I'm understanding a lot more now.
> A: What, in your opinion, needs to happen yet for you to become a Christian?

B: I'm not sure. I guess I just need to decide to let Christ come
    into my life.
A: Are you willing to do that?
B: Yes, I think I am.
A: Would you know how to go about it?
B: I think so.
A: How would you feel if we settled the issue together right
    now? Or would you rather do it on your own?

AVOID THE TIME PANIC.

Mother O'Leary's cow has had a great influence on evangelism in America. The cow kicked over a lantern, starting the
great Chicago Fire in which many people perished. D. L.
Moody was conducting evangelistic meetings in the city when
the fire took place. Moved by the tragedy, he announced that
he would never again preach without giving an invitation.
Many ministers have picked up on Moody's commitment,
and on the level of personal evangelism many of us now
labor under an exaggerated sense of urgency. Often we fear
that if the person doesn't make a decision on the spot, he
never will. We fear that when he goes his way, still undecided,
he will probably be struck by a car—and then his blood will
be on our hands.

But anxieties of this sort come from a false sense of
responsibility. I am not the Lord of the harvest; *God* is. It is the
Holy Spirit who draws people to Christ. We can be confident
that He will preserve and complete His work in those who are
on the way, responding to Christ.

The gospel is urgent news, but that doesn't mean we
should be in the kind of time panic that can be so destructive
in its results! I have a friend who was led into a response at the
age of eight under the kind of pressure we are talking about.
For the next fifteen years he went through an incredible

inner struggle. Finally, at age twenty-three, he was able to recognize that the necessary inner transaction had never occurred. So we need patience. We need to believe that God will bring about conversion in its proper time.

SUMMARY SUGGESTIONS

Throughout the course of sowing and reaping in the harvest field, we should keep certain basic practical guidelines in mind:

Things to do—

- Accept the nonChristian as he is. Try to be a genuine friend.
- Maintain friendly contact between sessions, but don't overdo it. One friendly contact between sessions is usually sufficient.
- Keep it simple. Focus on the two basic questions.
- Keep the group homogeneous if it is a group study.
- Be sensitive about when to introduce the idea of the need for an eventual decision.
- Allow time for the "decision" idea to ferment.
- Make the actual "assist" after the Holy Spirit has done His work.

Things to avoid—

- Avoid attempting to reform the nonChristian.
- Avoid letting sessions drag on. It is better to quit too soon, leaving the people hungry.
- Avoid letting cancellations bother you. Respond with acceptance.
- Avoid worrying that progress is slow. Just keep the person in the Scriptures.
- Avoid being impatient for a decision. Remember that it takes time to overcome a rebellious will. Let the Holy Spirit do His work.

Results to expect—
- God will accomplish His purpose.
- The conversion will be genuine.
- Follow-up will be automatic as you continue.

NOTES
1. James F. Engel, *Contemporary Christian Communications* (Nashville: Thomas Nelson Publishers, 1979), page 75.
2. Engel, page 98.

12
Enlarging Your Circles of Opportunity

Inherent in man is a craving for involvement in things of significance. There is nothing more significant or more adventurous than participating in the purposes of God—sharing in finishing His work. His work has to do with people.

This book is written on the assumption that healthy Christians desire meaningful involvement with people in evangelism. It also assumes that such involvement is within our reach. Jesus expressed feelings of personal fulfillment after talking to the Samaritan woman. "I have food to eat that you know nothing about. . . . My food," said Jesus, "is to do the will of him who sent me and to finish his work" (John 4:32,34). Jesus had been fed well by His conversation.

As Christians we have a natural concern for evangelism. But most of us have some personal adjustments to make if we are to become meaningfully involved with nonChristians. I have described these adjustments relating to the work of evangelism in the preceding pages of this book. Here they are in review:

- We should overcome our initial inertia by committing ourselves to action and changing our living patterns.
- We should gain an understanding of the people of our time and learn to relate to them accordingly.
- We should acquire new skills in communication.
- We should get our nonChristian friends involved in an ongoing exposure to the Scriptures.

DON'T SPEND YOUR
LIFETIME STARTING OVER.

Once we are moving in these areas, we don't want to lose our hard-won momentum. Evangelism should become a continuous, integral part of our lifestyle. Often our first crisis in this area comes as a result of our success. Our nonChristian friends have come to know Christ. What is the next step? Do we begin all over again making new acquaintances and building new relationships so that once again we can sit down with a nonChristian over an open Bible?

A lifetime of repeating this lengthy and laborious process would be difficult to live with. In fact, if this kind of repetition is necessary, then we are certainly doing something wrong, failing to capitalize on the natural opportunities inherent in each situation. Usually when initial relationships have been established and people begin to respond to Christ, one relationship leads to another. The succeeding concentric circles of opportunity can continue almost indefinitely.

We need to use wisdom, however, if our opportunities

are to expand in this way. It is our challenge to help the new Christian integrate into the Body of Christ in such a way that he preserves his communication with his peers and family in the process.

The new Christian meets the church—The new Christian's first exposure to the local church can be a very delicate encounter! On one occasion I was invited to address this subject at a conference for missionaries of a particular denomination. They explained their situation as follows: "We are relatively successful in evangelism. Our difficulty lies in getting converts into our churches. We lose most of them at that point." This is one of the most common difficulties the Church encounters around the world.

The degree of success in bringing new Christians out of the world and into our existing church fellowships depends on a number of factors: the spiritual vigor of the local fellowship; the relevance of the forms of the local church to those who are coming in; the nature of the evangelism employed; the background of the people coming to Christ; and the distance between the church's "culture" and the culture of the new Christians.

I marvel at the apparent ease with which first-century churches incorporated their new converts. The churches were very indigenous or "grassroots." These early churches were natural to the culture in which they flourished. They met primarily in homes. Once the initial beachhead was established through the apostolic effort, the churches grew because of the influence of the believers on those around them. Structures, or forms, were relevant because they were created in response to immediate needs. It is interesting that the New Testament doesn't even address the question of how to get converts into a church. To be converted was to be in!

Perhaps we need to make a 180 degree turn in our

thinking on this matter, particularly in situations where the distances are really great between two cultures. Should we continue to think in terms of taking the new Christian to church, or should we think of bringing the church to him? The church is not a physical structure; it is people. It consists of Christians relating in such a way that they help one another live the Christian life. A church building is not required to meet the spiritual needs of a body of new Christians.

If we think "people" when we think "church," then we can have the necessary flexibility to incorporate those we win, without dislocating them at all. As more of their kind come to Christ, and as they are supported and ministered to by people sent out by the local church, their Body-needs begin to be met. Whether this arrangement is provisory or becomes permanent (as in the case of a mini-church or satellite church), it offers two immediate advantages. First, the new Christian has plenty of time to mature spiritually in surroundings that he has already accepted. With this maturity, he will gain a tolerance for further adaptation. Second, in leaving him where he is, we are not cutting him off from his natural network of relationships.

So I'm suggesting we not be in a hurry to tie new Christians into our traditional congregational structures, especially those converts coming out of a highly secularized context. I am also saying there will be situations where the distances will be so great that we should simply accept the fact that new wineskins will be needed.

Expectations on Christian conduct—By insisting on conformity in gray areas of conduct, we might quickly terminate the new Christian's communication within his old network of relationships. Thus we must differentiate between behavior that is nonnegotiable (what is right and what is wrong) and behavior that has no hard and fast ethical guidelines.

The Bible instructs us on several categories of behavior. Certain things are always right. Whatever the situation, if you do these things your behavior will be correct. Galatians 5:22-23 gives us a sample list: love, joy, peace, patience, kindness, goodness, faithfulness, gentleness, and self-control. There are no laws against any of these characteristics. So the first category of behavior consists of those qualities the Bible specifically identifies as right behavior.

Then this same passage specifies certain behavior as always wrong. No matter what the situation, it's wrong. Sexual immorality, impurity, hatred, discord, jealousy, fits of rage, selfish ambition, envy, drunkenness, and so on, are out (Galatians 5:19-21). They have no place in the life of any Christian at any time.

Although certain matters of conduct are clear-cut, there is an in-between category of "disputable matters" (Romans 14:1). These are areas the Bible does not specifically address—matters such as what day to worship or what foods to eat. What constitutes proper behavior in this case is determined by several variable factors. Sometimes it might be wrong to do a particular thing. But at other times that same action might be right. The Bible leaves it up to the individual believer to decide *what* is proper for him, and also *when* and *where*.

This rather open arrangement is considered too ambiguous and risky for many church bodies to contemplate. Conformity of behavior is easier to live with. Nonconformity, we reason, tends to engender judgments and conflicts. Thus we find it safer to define a position on the more bothersome, doubtful issues, and then we ask everyone to fall in line. The Bible instructs us *not* to handle doubtful issues this way, but we do it anyway (Romans 14:1-4, 22; Colossians 2:16, 20-23).

According to Romans 14, one of the signs of a healthy fellowship is a loving attitude toward diversity of convictions on those matters of personal behavior that are relative and not absolute. The mature know the kingdom of God does not consist of eating and drinking. Consequently, they accept the various behavioral choices on doubtful issues without judging. They know that in the end all accounts will be settled individually before God Himself. So they make room for the scrupulous, and accept the uninhibited as well. Their own behavior is ruled by the laws of love and moderation (Romans 13:10, 1 Corinthians 9:24-27).

In a group where these principles prevail, there will be room for new Christians to be accepted as they grow into their own convictions. This makes for greater maturity in the long run (Hebrews 5:14).

How we handle this matter of doubtful things will heavily influence the nature and extent of our outreach. Frequently new Christians are cut off from their nonChristian peers when they conform to the extra-biblical standards that their newly adopted Christian community imposes on them. Because of such rules, new Christians suddenly discover that their old friends are off-limits. When this happens, we are back to where we started, looking for new threads that will lead us into new relationships, etc.

CO-LABORING WITH OUR SPIRITUAL CHILDREN

We are able to have an ongoing, fruitful ministry among people in the mainstream only to the degree that we are able to extend our witness to the network of relationships of the people we have already reached. We must not inadvertently and unnecessarily cut off communication within this network.

It is vitally important to help the new Christian coming

from the world to integrate into the Church. It is obvious that coming to Christ means a break with the past, a new beginning. But this is a repudiation of the *works* of the past, not the *people* of the past. That's why we need to keep these two elements in perspective.

As our opportunities expand, with one relationship leading to another, we need to co-labor with those we are ministering to. We need their help, and they need ours.

NonChristians can be great evangelists.—This is an overstatement, but it makes the point. Frequently people who are discovering the Bible for the first time and are on their way toward Christ show a fresh, uninhibited enthusiasm over their new discoveries.

One new Christian with whom I'm currently involved brought at least a dozen people around before he himself believed. He often brought his friends with him to our studies. Then, with his typical lack of inhibition, he would inject articulate questions and doubts about God and about this world He has created. This was distressing only to the person trying to lead the discussion. His guests, rather than being driven to doubt by his performances, were made to feel at home. Unintentionally, he was expressing their questions as well.

People don't need to know much before they can begin to influence others. Philip brought Nathanael to Jesus with three words: "Come and see" (John 1:46). The Samaritan woman did the same with her neighbors: "Come, see a man who told me everything I ever did. Could this be the Christ?" (John 4:29).

We shouldn't overlook the potential for outreach the nonChristian can offer. We should encourage him in this by affirming his efforts and by being careful to respect the needs and feelings of his friends when he brings them around.

New Christians can be very bad evangelists.—For some reason, once a person crosses the line of belief, he frequently goes through a period when he loses this ability to draw others in. Things get awkward. The new Christian can be very overbearing and dogmatic among his friends, and especially with his family. He tends to say too much, press too hard, and he can't understand why everyone in the world can't see something that has become so obvious to him. He tends to forget that it took him many years to see it himself.

Much permanent damage can be done in the first few weeks of a person's Christian life. He can burn off his communication with his peers. Then, smarting from the ensuing rejection, he can conclude that evangelism is something to be carefully avoided in the future.

Thus, new Christians need coaching. They need to be made aware of the things mentioned here. They need to be encouraged to share their faith, but they also need help in what and how much to say. They need to learn the essential message of "evangelism as a lifestyle," that evangelism is more than the verbal witness. If they have been brought to Christ through the process of *affirmation* that we have been describing, it will be easier for them to understand that the same kind of process is necessary among their peers.

Extend your friendship.—When a person coming to Christ realizes that you will extend your love and acceptance to his friends without seizing the first opportunity to assault them with the gospel, then he will want to bring them around. But until he is sure it is safe, he won't.

We should be prepared to keep social occasions strictly social and not to think in terms of using them as bait for a session in the Bible. I had to blunder on this one a number of times before one nonChristian finally confronted me, charging me with being deceitful. We get much further with people when we are honest and up-front with our intentions. A social occasion should be a social occasion. When we intend to open the Bible with people, our invitation should communicate this intention.

We should not feel the evening was wasted when the dinner conversation didn't lead into a verbal witness of some kind. If we are light, the non-verbal witness will be communicated. Mini-decisions *will* be made, and once there is some foundation of confidence, the relationship will support the weight of the verbal witness. This building of confidence will take far less time among our friends' friends, because we will in a sense be hitchhiking on longstanding relationships.

A word of caution is needed at this point. We are talking about extending the outreach of the gospel throughout the spheres of influence of those we reach. We need to be careful of the form this takes. The temptation is to usurp the opportunities as our own, to make the process a simple extension of our own evangelism. In fact, the new Christian will often initiate this himself, bringing his friends for us to evangelize. But to do this evangelism ourselves would be to miss the greatest opportunity inherent in the situation, that of multiplying our ministry by training the new Christian in evangelism. We need to make sure that he is always involved in the process as a co-laborer, assuming more and more direct responsibility as he matures. As the concentric circles of opportunity expand, the number of evangelists multiplies accordingly.

Provide a bridge into the gospel.—Evangelism in Ephesus took a fascinating form. The apostle Paul began in the synagogue. When the conflict with the Jews became too heavy, he moved to a neutral location, taking his disciples with him. He conducted daily discussions in the school of Tyrannus for two years (Acts 19:8-10). The result was that "all the Jews and

Greeks who lived in the province of Asia heard the word of the Lord." What were those discussions like? How were they conducted? What did they talk about? We'll never know. We only know that they were dynamic. Otherwise the whole province of Asia wouldn't have bothered to listen.

It is useful to observe that these daily discussions provided a forum where people could come and listen, interact, go away and think—and then come back for more. Certainly the discussions became known by word of mouth by those who had come to faith or were on their way. The ongoing exposure to the gospel had a cumulative effect in the region.

Only an unusually gifted teacher could attempt to do something as far-reaching as Paul's teaching in Ephesus. But we can achieve a similar effect, at whatever level the abilities of our little band of kindred spirits permits. The school of Tyrannus was essentially a neutral place (in contrast to the synagogue) where interested people could receive an ongoing exposure to the message.

There are ways in which we can provide a similar opportunity, even on a one-on-one basis. For example, we can maintain an open-door attitude toward the friends of the people with whom we are currently involved in the Scriptures. So what if someone new drops in at chapter five? A quick review that brings him up to date will benefit everyone.

Another way to create an environment where young Christians can help bridge the gap between their friends and the gospel is to conduct a series of three or four open discussions on some deeply felt need (see Chapter 8). If it is beyond your abilities to do this among yourselves, invite someone in to teach. It would be better, however, for you or someone in your group to go to a person who can give you the help you need to prepare to do it yourself. This would be an opportunity for you to learn and develop.

Pick an area or topic of interest. Study it; read up on it.

Take your time, and when your thoughts are in order and in communicable form, then proceed. Invite a number of non-Christians equivalent to the present number in your group.

Begin with a twenty to thirty minute presentation designed to give a foundation of biblical thought on the subject and to stimulate discussion. Discussion is stimulated by creating tension—positive tension, of course. Good questions create this kind of tension. Have a few guide questions prepared to keep things moving, and then be ready with a closing summary. When you're done, break for coffee and an informal time together.

Here are some possible topics:
- God and history: What does the Bible say about current events? About the future?
- What does the Bible say about marriage? About the family? About child rearing?
- What is success? How is it achieved and maintained?
- Biblical principles of financial management.
- Interpersonal relationships.

The purpose of open discussions like these is not to bring people to the point of decision but to bring them to see that a relationship with God is fundamental to living and understanding life. Such discussions should motivate people to respond to our invitation to go on to examine the Bible further with us. One of the positive effects of these discussions will be that we have provided our new co-laborers with the assistance they need to draw their friends into a meaningful exposure to Christians and to the Christian message.

Epilogue

This book has focused on one of the essential functions of the Church: evangelism. Since it is impossible to isolate evangelism from its adjoining functions of establishing, edifying, and equipping Christians for the ministry, I fear that I have raised as many questions as I may have answered. This is due to the fact that I have limited the scope of this book not only to evangelism but also to a particular form of evangelism, one that meets two basic needs: (1) The need to communicate the gospel to the people who are caught up in the mainstream of our society, those who are being carried in the opposite direction, away from Christian presuppositions and values; and (2) The need for a concept of evangelism that provides meaningful, ongoing involvement for the average Christian among his peers. The questions raised have contextual answers.

I would like to think that after reading these pages the reader's reaction will be, "I can do that! With a little help from my friends, I can do it." I hope this book gives enough guidance and answers enough questions to bring the reader to this conclusion.

This book raises questions about the implications of our success in reaching people of the mainstream. Generally we're not accustomed to such secularized people coming into the Body. How do we minister to these people whose needs and values are so different from our own? How do we accommodate this kind of growth into the Body?

For now, let's press ahead, concentrating on bringing these questions upon us! The fruit of our labors will transform what are now theoretical questions into real needs. This will enable us to define them accurately and resolve them biblically and practically. Necessity fathers creativity.

A FINAL WORD

After investing fourteen long years in ministry among the Gentiles, the apostle Paul returned to Jerusalem to consult with the men in leadership there (Galatians 2:1-10). He did this, he said, "for fear that I was running or had run my race in vain."

Isn't it strange that Paul, after experiencing God's great blessings on his efforts, worried that it could all prove to be in vain? What were his misgivings? He had no doubt about his message! He had just finished saying, "If anybody is preaching to you a gospel other than what you accepted, let him be eternally condemned!" (Galatians 1:9).

Paul's doubts were over how his brothers were feeling

about what he was doing. He wanted to be sure they understood and accepted his relatively off-beat ministry among the Gentiles. He wanted their approval and support. He was concerned about *unity*.

Unity is not uniformity. In this encounter Paul and Barnabas agreed with Peter, James, and John that the most effective thing would be to maintain the diversity. "They agreed that we should go to the Gentiles, and they to the Jews" (Galatians 2:9). So there was diversity in what they did and how they did it, but there was unity of mind and purpose regarding their overall mission.

We have been talking about taking the gospel to a diversified and diversifying world. There are countless cultures and subcultures among the nearly 4.5 billion people in the world, and many trends within each of these cultures! To go as a Church to this world and to cope with this diversity without making unwholesome judgments and comparisons will take a miracle of God's grace.

On the individual level, we want to commit ourselves to maintaining an attitude of humble submission to our pastors, spiritual overseers, and brothers as we move into the spheres of ministry we have examined in this book. To do otherwise is to run the risk of laboring in vain. Wherever love does not prevail between brothers we essentially deny the gospel. We rob it of its credibility and power, destroying the very thing we have purposed to build. Jesus said, "All men will know that you are my disciples if you love one another" (John 13:35).

APPENDIX:

Twenty-four Hours with John

Twenty-four Hours with John

From a strictly historical point of view, Jesus of Nazareth was the most remarkable person in all human history. Whatever people's opinions of Him may be, almost everyone would seize an opportunity to spend a day with one of His closest friends.

The apostle John was among Jesus' three closest friends. He was in on everything. Frequently it would be just the four of them together: Jesus, Peter, James, and John. John saw Jesus, touched Him, heard Him speak. Together they walked the hot dusty roads—conversing, perspiring, experiencing hunger and thirst.

John recorded many of his experiences with Jesus. As he

put it, "We proclaim to you what we have seen and heard, so that you also may have fellowship with us" (1 John 1:3).

John's record of his encounters with Jesus, the Gospel of John, is divided into twenty-one chapters. This Bible study is a total of twenty-four lessons. Two of the chapters are so long that I divided each of them into two lessons. Also, I have included a summary study with an illustration that summarizes John's central message, which happens to be the central message of the whole Bible. These twenty-four studies offer us an opportunity to spend twenty-four hours with John.

As you, the leader, guide the nonChristian into this adventure with John, it will be important to keep certain things in mind. We have already discussed most of these points in this book, but we will review them here.

1. Remember that your part of the process in evangelism is to love the individual and help him understand what the Bible says. Leave the rest to the Holy Spirit and the Word of God.

2. Since the primary issue for the nonChristian is the matter of Jesus' identity, this is where we want to focus our attention in these studies. We can summarize the scope of our emphasis with just two questions: (a) Who is Jesus? and (b) What does He want of me?

3. Don't feel you need to rigidly follow the questions I have provided here. Discussions never go quite the way we intend. The objective is not to cover all the material; it is simply to help the other person understand what each chapter says.

4. You don't want to walk into an evangelistic study with this book in one hand and a Bible in the other. I have always felt uneasy about using any printed materials while studying with truly secularized people. To them, the printed page often smells of indoctrination. It's better to write out on a separate piece of paper the

questions and cross references you intend to use. This, I find, contributes to the spontaneity of the discussions.

5. Seldom will it take all twenty-four studies for a non-Christian to come to faith. How long it will take depends on the distance the person is from Christ and the nature of the obstacles he has to overcome. So what do you do if a person becomes a Christian while you are studying Chapter 6? You go on to Chapter 7.

The whole Christian life can be summarized in our two questions: Who is Jesus? What does He want of me? All of us would do well to dedicate our lives to answering these two questions.

So when a person comes to faith in the midst of these studies, just keep going. Rejoice with him over his spiritual birth, and then proceed, paying special attention to the second question: What does He want of me? The Gospel of John contains some of the greatest "follow-up material" ever written.

6. Remember that at the beginning your friend is committed to you for only one study at a time. Even in later stages only you will be aware of the extensiveness of the process.

This material is intended as a guide for you, not for the other person. He probably should not even be aware of its existence. This will give you the freedom to select what you need out of these studies. Use your own judgment in deciding what and how much you will use.

The Gospel of John:
A Bible Study

STUDY #1—JOHN 1:1-14

1. What is John referring to when he speaks of the "Word" in verses 1,2,3, and 14? (See 1 John 1:1-3).

2. Why is Christ called the Word? What is the use of a word among people? Supposing that God exists, how might one come to know Him? (John 1:18, 14:6). What are the implications of Christ's declaration in John 14:6?

   Note: Since He polarized the options with this statement, He was either the legitimate Messiah or a blatant fraud.

3. What qualities are attributed to the Word in 1:1-5, 14?

4. Another analogy is used to describe Christ in 1:4-9. What is it? What is the function of a light? Why is Jesus called "the light of men"? (1:4).

5. What are the implications of this title? (See 3:19-21, 8:12, and 12:35-36).

6. In what sense are all men illuminated by the Light? (1:4,9).

   Note: All people are created by Him. All have *life* from Him. But man has abandoned this source of life and has fallen into darkness. There are still traces in man of his noble origin, but they are merely the remains of what he once was. What does remain?

   > A *certain God-consciousness*—Everyone has a certain knowledge of God, in the same way that something may be known about an artist by seeing his works (See Romans 1:18-21).
   > An *innate sense of morality*—Everyone has an idea of how life should work: the "internal laws" (See Romans 2:14-15).

   These two elements explain the existence of religions and philosophies: a "God" notion and a standard of morality of which this God is the guardian. However, it is only by returning to the Light that man can be illuminated and thereby reoriented. Life is in Him. We understand life—our own and others'—by coming to the Light.

7. According to 1:11-13, how does a person enter God's family?

   Note: It does *not* happen through heredity, self-effort, or someone else's effort (pastor, priest, etc.).

8. What do you think it means to "receive Christ"?

Note: In 1:12, "receive" and "believe" are synonymous. In John 3:36, the opposite of believing is rebellion against God—not accepting His authority over our lives. What do you conclude from this? Belief implies submission (See Revelation 3:20).

STUDY #2—JOHN 1:15-51

A. John 1:15-28

1. What does John say about Christ in 1:15?

2. What law did Moses give? (1:17). Why was it given?

Note: The law wasn't given to be kept, but to reveal the sin in man. Like an x-ray, it doesn't cure anything; it simply reveals the problem. (See Romans 3:19-20, Galatians 2:16, 3:24, and John 5:45.)

3. According to John 1:23, what was the primary role of John the Baptist? (See also John 3:26-30, 7:29-30, and Luke 3:4-14).

Note: John the Baptist announced the imminent arrival of the Messiah, calling on men to make their way straight—a way that had been twisted by centuries of self-will and religious traditions. If they didn't do this, they wouldn't recognize the Messiah.

How could the people of Israel straighten their way of living?

Note: Repentance means a change in mentality, a desire to leave your current way of life in order to enter into a relationship with Christ. Notice that the change came first, then the baptism. The act of baptism was the sign that the individual had indeed repented (See Luke

3:4-14). Baptism is the audiovisualization of the Message. It doesn't give life. It only indicates, "I'm one of them," displaying this internal desire for change.

B. John 1:29-34

4. Why was Jesus called the "Lamb of God"? (See Isaiah 53:4-7 and Hebrews 9:11-28).

Note: The Old Testament sacrifices are illustrations of the need for the single, sufficient sacrifice of Christ.

5. What are the implications of John the Baptist's declaration in 1:33 that Jesus would baptize with the Holy Spirit?

Note: Being a Christian isn't merely following a certain philosophy or becoming part of a religious system. It is a relationship between two persons, Jesus Christ and the individual, as well as the spontaneous change this relationship causes within the individual (See 1:12, 3:5-8, and 4:23-24).

C. John 1:35-51

6. This section relates the stories of five people and the way they came to know and trust in Christ, each one by a different means. Who are they and what led them to believe in Christ?

STUDY #3—JOHN 2

A. John 2:1-11

1. What do you think Jesus' acceptance of the wedding invitation indicates? (See Matthew 11:16-19).

2. What problem was brought to Jesus during the celebration? How did He resolve it? Do you find this believable?

Note: What claim was made about Jesus in John 1:3? It would be hard to imagine the Creator appearing on earth without revealing His power over His creation. Christ, fully understanding the nature of matter and having power over it, could command it at will (See Hebrews 11:3).

3. Notice that John consistently uses the word "sign" instead of "miracle" (See 2:11). Why? What was the function of signs? (See 3:2 and 6:26).

4. Did Jesus fulfill His mother's request? Then how do you explain this dialogue between Him and His mother? (2:4-5).

    Note: "Woman" was an expression of endearment (See 19:26). This dialogue could be paraphrased as follows: "We are not of the same worlds. What is a problem for you isn't one for Me. I'll take care of it. I have time for such things before My 'hour' comes."

5. What did Jesus mean when He said, "My time has not yet come"? Who determines what is to be done when? (See 7:6, 8:20, 12:23,27, and 17:1).

    Note: Jesus' death was not a futile, unforeseen tragedy. It was the reason for His coming. The signs He performed contributed to setting off the chain-reaction-like process that inevitably led to His death.

B. John 2:12-22

6. What led Jesus to act the way He did when He cleared the temple? (2:13-17).

    Note: The Passover was one of the principal religious feasts of the Jews. They came to Jerusalem for celebration and spiritual cleansing. However, the temple merchants were exploiting the situation by selling animals and exchanging foreign currencies for the temple currency— all for a nice profit. Jesus accused them of soiling God's name. He told them, in so many words, "Don't use My Father's name to promote your dirty business!" (See Romans 2:24).

How can Jesus' anger be justified? Did He lose His head? Why didn't anyone fight back?

7. How did Jesus respond to the Jews' demand to show them His credentials, His authority for doing such things? (2:18-22).

Note: Jesus responded with His own demand: "Kill Me! Then I'll show you who I am!" (See 1 Corinthians 15:12-19.) Christ's resurrection is fundamental in settling the issue of His "credentials." If He didn't rise from the dead, then it is all a fraud. And what does it mean if He did rise from the dead?

C. John 2:23-25

8. The people believed in Jesus, but He didn't approve of their belief. Why?

Note: Real belief implies commitment and surrender. Their acceptance of Jesus did not include this kind of dedication. (See John 12:42-43 and James 2:19.) A faith in which the individual reserves the right to run his own life is not faith at all. (See John 3:36.)

STUDY #4—JOHN 3

A. John 3:1-15

1. What observations did Nicodemus make about Jesus? (3:1-2).

2. How did Jesus correct Nicodemus? When is someone qualified to understand the things of God? (See 1 Corinthians 2:7-16 and John 1:12-13).

Note: Jesus said that Nicodemus could not come to any meaningful conclusions about the things of God without being "born again."

3. In what ways did it become evident that Nicodemus did not understand spiritual matters? (3:4,9).

Note: God speaks on a spiritual level. Man interprets Him on human terms and finds it difficult to conceive of anything beyond those terms. For example, imagine a world of blind men attempting to comprehend the color red. Their failure to comprehend it does not preclude its existence. To "see" the kingdom of God, one must acquire spiritual senses.

4. Why does Jesus insist that one must be born all over again before he can belong to God's kingdom? (John 3:3,5,8). (See also Ephesians 2:1-9.)

Note: Since the natural man is dead due to his sin, he must be born again to receive what he does not have: life.

What does being "born of water" mean? (John 3:5).

Note: Jesus was probably referring to the baptism of John here. (That was the only kind of "water" Nicodemus was acquainted with.) However, this does not imply that one must be baptized to be saved. John's baptism was a symbol of repentance already in effect. (See Luke 3:7-14.)

The water didn't bring about the change; the repentance did it. Repentance is necessary if spiritual birth is to take place (See Luke 13:1-5 and Isaiah 53:6). Jesus was saying to Nicodemus, "Do what John the Baptist has said. Do an about-face, leaving your old way of thinking; then permit the Holy Spirit to enter you, giving you a new life."

By itself, John's message of repentance was not complete. It was not sufficient for spiritual life without the additional part of being "born of the Spirit." (See Acts 19:1-7.)

5. What does Jesus mean by being "born again"? (See Luke 6:43-45).
   Note: The only way to change the kind of fruit a tree produces is to graft in a new branch. How does this happen? (See John 1:12-13).

B. John 3:16-36

6. The word *believe* appears several times in verses 15-18. What is the relationship between believing and being born again? (3:15).

7. For what purpose did God send Christ? Why? (3:16-21).

8. How can one be certain that God is real? (John 3:31-33 and 7:17).

9. What did you learn about your relationship with God from the study of this chapter?

STUDY #5—JOHN 4

A. John 4:1-18

1. Jesus offered "living water" to the Samaritan woman (4:10). What claims did He make about this very special water?

2. What did He mean by "living water"? (See Isaiah 44:3-4 and John 7:37-39).

3. What is this "thirst"? (4:14).

> *Note:* The innate human dissatisfaction is strong.

> How had the woman previously tried to quench her thirst?

> *Note:* She had been drinking at the wrong fountain— the fountain of promiscuity (4:17-18). (See also Isaiah 55:1-2.)

4. Why didn't the woman understand what Jesus meant by living water?

> *Note:* She was thinking in the natural plane, whereas Jesus was speaking of the supernatural (John 3:4; 6:26,34).

B. John 4:19-30

5. As soon as the Samaritan woman perceived that the conversation was heading toward religion, she tried to keep it from becoming personal by employing a very common tactic. What was it? (4:19-20).

> *Note:* She tried to draw Jesus into a general discussion on religion, but one that didn't focus on her.

> How did Jesus handle her evasive tactic? (4:21-24).

> *Note:* It's not the religious system, or the forms, or the creed that makes the difference. God's new temple is the individual, and that is where the worship is to take place (1 Corinthians 6:19).

6. Jesus faced the woman with a decision (4:26). What was it?

C. John 4:31-38

7. Why was Jesus no longer hungry? (See 4:31-34).

> What is the harvest? (4:35). (See also Matthew 9:36-38.) Who are the harvesters? (See 2 Corinthians 5:18-20). Who are the reapers? (4:36-38). (See also John 4:14 and 2 Corinthians 5:18-20.)

D. John 4:46-54

8. Why didn't Jesus accept the royal official's faith? What was the difference between his attitude and that of the official in Matthew 8:8?

How did Christ help this royal official come to the kind of faith that truly makes a difference in one's life? (4:50-53). (See also Acts 27:25.)

STUDY #6—JOHN 5

A. John 5:1-18— (Note: The most ancient known documents do not include verse 4. This suggests that it may have been interpolated later to explain the phenomenon of the pool.)

1. Why did Jesus choose that particular lame man out of the multitude of diseased people? (5:7). (See also Luke 19:10.)
   Did the lame man demonstrate any faith?

2. Imagine being a paralyzed beggar waiting thirty-eight years for an improbable cure. Yet Jesus spoke of "something worse" (5:14). What could it be? (See Matthew 16:26).

3. Is it possible to quit sinning? (See Romans 2:12).
   Then why did Jesus tell him to stop? (See Romans 3:19-31).
   Note: Imagine how the man felt when he found himself sinning again after Jesus' warning. But he had to try to stop on his own to be convinced that he couldn't stop. It usually takes such a stubborn independent attempt before we try God's way. The man had to realize that it was impossible for him not to sin unless he changed his very nature. He had to be born again (John 3:3).

4. Why did Jesus deliberately violate the Sabbath? (5:16-18). (See also Mark 2:23-28 and Matthew 12:1-14.)

Note: Centuries of tradition carried the Jews further and further from what the Old Testament actually taught regarding the Sabbath. Jesus was merely giving the Sabbath its proper interpretation. Tradition for the sake of tradition creates deterioration. (See Mark 7:6-9.)

5. What claim did Jesus make about Himself? (5:17-18).

B. John 5:19-30

6. What kind of relationship did Jesus have with His Father? In what sense was He dependent on Him? (See 8:28, 12:48-49, and 14:10).

7. What three promises did Jesus make? (5:24). According to this verse, what must one do to receive these promises?

8. Verse 29 seems to contradict the teaching that spiritual life comes through faith and not through works. How can this be reconciled?

Note: The life must come first. It is the life that produces the works. (See John 6:28-29 and 15:5.)

C. John 5:31-47

9. Jesus presented five witnesses who attested to His deity (5:31-39). Who were they?

> *Note:* a. Jesus Himself
> b. His own works
> c. John the Baptist
> d. The Father
> e. The Scriptures

It is possible to isolate these witnesses, casting doubt on them individually. But when they are called to the stand together, although they do not prove the divinity of Christ in human proofs, they become irrefutable.

10. What obstacle to faith is mentioned in 5:44? (See also 12:43.) Do people still have this sort of problem?

STUDY #7—JOHN 6

A. John 6:1-30

1. What motivated the multitudes to follow Jesus? (6:2,14-15, 26-27).

> *Note:* a. Their physical problems
> b. Politics
> c. Material gain (free bread)

Do these same things motivate people to be religious today?

2. How did Jesus react to these people? (6:26-29).

> *Note:* He rejected them. What was it that disqualified them? They refused to accept the significance of the signs. They sought personal advantage, not Christ Himself.

B. John 6:31-51

3. What was Jesus trying to teach the crowd when He fed them bread? (6:27). (See also Isaiah 55:1-2.) What does this bread and manna signify?

4. Could Jesus, if He were merely a teacher or philosopher, have given the discourse found in 6:35-38?

> a. What did He imply when He referred to Himself as the "Bread of Life"? (6:33, 51).
>
> > *Note:* He is from the supernatural world (6:38,41-42). He gives life to the world (6:33). He satisfies peo-

ple's hunger and thirst (6:35). He is eternal (6:51,54).

b. How can you get some of this bread into the current realities of your life? (6:51-58).

c. What did Jesus mean by the phrase "eat my flesh and drink my blood"?

Note: It is an individual act. We must take Christ in as the "staff of life." (See Galatians 2:20.) This chapter is not directly referring to Communion. With whom did Jesus break bread at the Lord's Supper? For what purpose? (See Luke 22:14-23). The Lord's Supper was intended to provide a permanent remembrace of the hour of His death. Jesus told the multitude in John 6 that they had to eat and drink of Him for a very different reason. What was it?

C. John 6:52-65

5. Why didn't Jesus try to smooth things over when He saw that His followers were offended by what He said? (6:60-66). (See also Matthew 15:8-9 and Acts 28:26-27.)

Note: The people were only superficially accepting Jesus. But He wanted all or nothing. He did those people a favor by sending them away. They had long been under the illusion that they were "followers of Christ." But His nonnegotiable terms are, "Give Me your whole self or forget it!"

D. John 6:66-71

6. When Jesus asked His twelve disciples why they didn't leave along with everyone else, Peter summed up their position (6:68-69). What was his answer?

7. What new and challenging principles have you learned about being a follower of Jesus Christ through the study of this chapter?

STUDY #8—JOHN 7

The primary theme of this chapter is the controversy that continually stirred in first-century Israel over the question, "Who is He?"

1. List the factors that contributed to the bafflement of the people on this question, as indicated in the following verses:
   John 7:14-15—
   John 7:19-20—
   John 7:25-27—
   John 7:31—
   John 7:40-44—
   John 7:46-49—
   John 7:52—

2. Did you notice the extent of their confusion resulting from their preconceived notions about the Messiah? Where did these preconceptions originate?

   Note: Luke 24:25-27—Ignorance of the Scriptures and/or failure to understand them. Mark 7:7-9—Religious traditions.

   Do you have similar misconceptions to deal with before you can come to understand Jesus Christ?

3. What positive evidence is given in this chapter for the deity of Jesus Christ?

   Note: John 7:15-16, 46—His wisdom
   John 7:28-29—What He Himself claimed to be
   John 7:31—His signs
   John 7:33-34—His prediction of His resurrection
   John 7:37-39—His claims to give life to others
   John 7:41-42—The prophets

4. In John 7:37-39, Jesus issued an offer.
   a. To whom did He make it?
   b. What kind of thirst was He talking about? (See John 4:13-14, 6:35, and Isaiah 55:1-3).
   c. Exactly what was He offering? (See John 14:25-26 and Romans 8:9).
   d. How does one respond to this offer? (See Revelation 3:20).

5. The guards were impressed with Christ's words. How did the authorities try to diminish this impression? (7:48-49).

6. What point was raised by Nicodemus, and how did the authorities react to it? (See 7:51-52 and Psalm 10:4).

STUDY #9—JOHN 8

A. John 8:1-11
1. Why did the Pharisees take the woman to Christ?

2. What was Jesus' attitude toward the woman caught in adultery? Did He approve of what she had done? Then why didn't He condemn her?
   Note: Was it that He closed His eyes to her sin? (See John 3:16-18 and 1 Peter 3:18). Jesus paid dearly to be able to offer her the pardon she needed. He took the woman's place. (See 2 Corinthians 5:21.)

3. In what way did Jesus try to help the Pharisees?
   Note: He tried to help them see that they were no different than the woman. But their case was more difficult. She knew she had a problem; they didn't. (See Mark 2:15-17 and Matthew 21:31-32.)

B. John 8:12-30

4. In 8:12, Jesus made another of His "I am" assertions. What was He saying when He referred to Himself as the "light of the world"? What does this imply for us? (See Ephesians 5:8-15).

5. In John 8:24, 28, and 58 we see more "I am" statements. To what was Jesus referring? I am *what?* He said that after His crucifixion people would know the answer to the question of His identity (8:28). What is the answer? (See Romans 5:8).

6. What was the main reason for the conflict between Jesus and His enemies? (8:23). Why is this so hard to accept?
   Note: To acknowledge Him would mean to admit they needed repentance. (See Luke 7:29-30.)

C. John 8:31-38

7. Jesus spoke of truth and freedom (8:31-36).
   a. What did He mean by "truth"?
      Note: What is a truth? Something tested and proven. Jesus said in John 14:6, "I am . . . the truth." Either this was the maximum expression of egotism— or He was right!
   b. How can we determine whether He was right or wrong? (8:31-32).
      Note: We must put Him to the test. . . on His terms.
   c. Jesus offered a spiritual maxim on freedom: Committing sin results in slavery (8:34). What does this mean?
      Note: The person who says, "I am free to do whatever my inner voice suggests," soon finds himself enslaved to what he sought to be free to do. (See Mark 7:14-23.) It is impossible to do or be what we really desire to do or be.

    d. In 8:33, note the symptom that people in spiritual slavery continually demonstrate.

        Note: They don't perceive their own slavery. (See John 9:39-41.)

    e. What must happen before a person can be really free?

        Note: Submitting to Christ requires an unconditional surrender (Luke 14:25-33). We must fully submit before He can do anything for us. Example: The sick must submit to the surgeon so that he can do whatever is necessary to produce the cure.

D. John 8:39-59

  8. Why did Jesus say that the Jews who rejected Him weren't sons of God? (John 8:42). How did He prove it? (8:37-47).

  9. Is it possible to believe in God and not believe in Christ? Why not? What are the characteristics of one who knows God and of one who doesn't?

 10. What was the Pharisees' conclusion by now of Jesus' identity? (8:48). How did they arrive at this conclusion? How did He answer them?

 11. List the main reasons from this chapter why it is of primary importance to establish a relationship with Jesus Christ.

STUDY #10—JOHN 9

The miracles Jesus performed were *signs* that pointed to the spiritual truths He sought to teach. The story of the blind man in this chapter is an example of this. By curing him, Jesus revealed what true blindness is, and who it is that is truly blind.

A. John 9:1-12

1. What was the disciples' evaluation of the blind man? (John 9:2).

2. What was Christ's evaluation of the blind man? (9:3).

   Note: He saw him as an opportunity to contribute to God's works. How does Christ interpret suffering? (See Romans 8:18-20 and Luke 13:1-5). The suffering we see in the world is a consequence of the fall. Those who believe participate in the damage just as those who don't believe. (See 2 Corinthians 12:8-10.) Suffering is an opportunity to allow God to manifest Himself.

3. What happened among the neighbors after the man was cured?

4. Did the ex-blind man's explanation satisfy them? Why not?

5. According to Jesus, what are the "works" of God? (See John 6:28-29,40).

B. John 9:13-34

6. How many times did the ex-blind man have to tell his story? Why?

7. Why was it so hard for others to accept the healing?
   a. The neighbors (9:13)
   b. The parents (9:22)
   c The Pharisees (9:16-19, 24, 29-34)

8. The neighbors, not satisfied, took the case to the theologians. What conclusion did they arrive at after examining the case theologically?

9. Why did their arguments fail to shake the ex-blind man? Who was in a better position to discuss the subject: the ex-blind man or the theologians?

   Note: Imagine trying to explain color to a blind man. You could not even prove that it exists. The blind man would probably even offer theoretical proofs as to why color can't exist. A simple beggar with eyesight would know more about color than the greatest intellectual blind man ever could.

10. Who finally won the argument? On what grounds?

11. How can the attitude of the parents of the blind man be explained? (See John 12:42-43).

C. John 9:35-41
12. How did the blind man become a Christian?

13. What must occur with each person in order to believe in Christ? (9:39-41).

14. Why weren't these Pharisees able to believe in Christ? Why is there more hope for those who admit blindness than for those who don't? (See Luke 5:30-32).

15. What is the parallel between this healing and the primary purpose of Christ's coming? (See Luke 4:16-22).

STUDY #11—JOHN 10

In this chapter we see Jesus as He describes the true leader and the false leader. The Scriptures frequently use a sheep-shepherd analogy in discussing leaders and followers. Why?

(See Psalm 100:3 and Matthew 9:36-39). Sheep can't survive without a shepherd. They are helpless.

A. John 10:1-18

1. This portion gives a parable and its explanation. What do you think is the main point of the parable?

   Note: Christ is the only one who takes a personal interest in man to the point of giving His life for him. (See also Psalm 100:3, Luke 15:4-7, 1 Peter 2:24-25, and Romans 8:31-39.)

2. What are the characteristics of a mercenary leader? (10:12-13). Whom would he represent?

   Note: He's not interested in the well-being of the individual. He's a professional, so to him man is just a means to an end. For this reason, when there is a crisis this type of leader leaves a man to his own plight.

   Read Ezekiel 34:1-31. Observe what this passage says about:
   a. The mercenary (verses 1-10)—the poor leader.
   b. The faithful shepherd (verses 11-16)—the good leader.
   c. The sheep (verses 16-31)—the kind of sheep the good leader is interested in.

3. In what way are sheep an apt analogy of men?

   Note: Read Isaiah 53:6, Jeremiah 10:23-24, and Matthew 10:36. Afflicted means no way out. Exhausted means without strength to resist.

4. What is the significance of Jesus' statement in verse seven that He is the "door" of the sheep? (See John 14:6). What kind of relationship is there between the sheep and Christ? (John 10:14-15). (See also John 17:3.)

5. What is the main characteristic of the person who is oriented by a faithful leader? (10:3-5, 16).

    Note: He heeds the shepherd and lives according to the orientation he receives from the shepherd.

B. John 10:19-42

6. In the remainder of this chapter, the perpetual question, "Who is this Jesus?" reappears. In how many ways did Jesus assert His deity in this section?

7. What does Christ offer to those who make the commitment to heed His Word?

    Note: Read 1 John 3:1-2, 2 Peter 1:4, and Romans 8:16-17, 28-30. Christ came to earth as the only begotten, the firstborn among many children of God who will share in a great eternal inheritance.

8. John 10:27-29 shows the security of the true Christian's position. What is the Christian's part in this? What is Christ's part?

9. Have you arrived at a personal conclusion on the question raised by the Jews? (10:24). What is the basis for your conclusion? What are the implications for your life in stating this conclusion?

STUDY #12—JOHN 11

A. John 11:1-17

1. Observe that Jesus deliberately delayed attending to the urgent request for help from His friends. The result was that Lazarus died before Jesus arrived there. Why did Jesus do this? (John 11:3-6, 11-15).

2. What did Christ want to communicate in the analogy of walking by day and walking by night? (9-10). (See also John 8:12, 9:4, and 13:27-30.) Whoever doesn't orient himself by God walks by night.

B. John 11:18-27

3. What are the implications of Jesus' assertion, "I am the resurrection and the life"? (11:25).

   Note: Read 1 Corinthians 15:12-19. *His* resurrection is the key to the resurrection He has promised *us*. (See 1 Corinthians 15:35-49.) What will be the nature of our resurrection?

4. What must happen to a person before he can share in this promise? (11:25-26).

   Note: Two grains of wheat may look exactly alike, but one may have the germ of life and the other may not. How does one acquire this germ of life? (See Romans 8:9-11).

C. John 11:28-46

5. Since Jesus knew that He would soon raise Lazarus from the dead, why then did He weep? (11:31-35, 41-44). (See also Luke 19:41-44.) He wept because of their unbelief.

D. John 11:47-57

6. What were the two different reactions to the miracle?

7. Normally unbelief is attributed to encountering things that are intellectually unacceptable. But on this occasion the unbelief appeared in the face of irrefutable evidence. What was the reason for rejecting Christ? (11:47-48). (See also John 12:9-11,42,43.) The reasons were political and social

8. Could these motives still be an obstacle today to people who are considering surrendering to Christ?

9. What was the human rationale used by the high priest Caiaphas to justify the plan to put a good man like Jesus to death? (11:49-50).

   How did this perspective coincide with God's eternal plan? (11:51-53). (See also Acts 2:22-23 and Isaiah 53:1-12.) Jesus' death was not an accident, nor a defeat at the hand of His enemies. It was the fulfillment of God's plan for the salvation of man.

STUDY #13—JOHN 12

A. John 12:1-11

1. Note who among the Twelve was the treasurer. Why do you suppose Jesus gave the job to the only thief in the group?

   Note: Judas needed an opportunity to see himself as he really was, so that he could be cured. (See Romans 7:7-8.)

2. What did Christ indicate by His answer that He knew about His near future? (12:7).

B. John 12:12-19

3. What led the crowd to give this demonstration? (12:17-18).

   Note: Jesus rejected the people's attempts to involve Him politically (John 6:14-18). Why, then, did He submit on this occasion? He was forcing a showdown. (See John 11:27-57.) By this act He demanded that the Jews make up their minds about Him: "Either accept Me as the Messiah or kill Me!" It was the last sign. (See Zechariah 9:9.)

4. What are the implications of Christ's claim for you personally? (12:13). What does the term "Rabbi" mean? (See Matthew 23:8). Can you call Him such a name?

C. John 12:20-36

5. According to these verses, what was Jesus' central purpose in life?

6. Christ said, "The hour has come for the Son of Man to be glorified" (12:23). What was He referring to? (See 12:27,32). Why was this His glorification? (See Exodus 33:18-19 and 1 Peter 2:24). The kindness, mercy, and compassion of God led Christ to take man's place on the Cross. That is the meaning of glorifying: showing who God is. Christ glorified the Father because He reflected the Father's character.

7. Who is "the prince of this world"? (12:31). (See also Luke 4:5-7.)
   What are the implications of this? (See Romans 8:18-22 and 1 John 5:19).

8. What lesson was Jesus teaching in His illustration about the grain of wheat? (12:24). How did His death bear much fruit? (See 1 Peter 2:24 and Romans 5:15-19). Why is this death indispensable? (See Luke 9:23-25).

9. In the subsequent verses, Jesus extends this principle of death as a prerequisite of fruitfulness to us as well. What do you understand about this?

D. John 12:37-50

10. Why is it that some people can't believe in Him?
    Note: What happens to those people who choose the

world's value system or refuse to give up their prejudices and their spiritual callousness? (See Acts 28:25-28). Do verses 38-40 suggest that some people can't be saved? (See 2 Corinthians 3:15-16).

STUDY #14—JOHN 13

A. John 13:1-20

1. Why didn't Peter want Jesus to wash his feet? (13:7-8, 12-14).

   Note: Washing feet in those days was the duty of a slave. Peter didn't understand what Jesus was teaching because he was thinking according to the world's value system.

   What was Christ totally aware of when He did this? (13:3).

2. Why did Peter change his mind, asking for a full bath? (13:8-9).

   Note: If having his feet washed would give Peter that kind of relationship with Christ, think of what it would mean to have a complete bath. Perhaps he was thinking of some sort of ritual that would assure him of a special relationship with Christ.

3. What was Jesus trying to teach His men by washing their feet?

   Note: Read Mark 10:35-45. Christ turns social ladders and organizational charts upside-down. This change in mentality is part of the process of the transformation that takes place when we follow Him.

   In what ways would the application of this principle change your life?

4. Why did Jesus say that Peter didn't need a complete bath? (13:10). (See also 1 Corinthians 6:11.)

Note: We need the daily cleansing Christ offers us because our feet are constantly contaminated by the dust of the world. (See Romans 12:1-2.)

5. Christ made two assertions (13:13). What are their implications for you?
   a. What does He mean by being our "Teacher"? Do you accept Him on this condition?
   b. What does He mean by being our "Lord"? Do you accept Him on this condition?

B. John 13:21-38

6. Why did Judas betray Christ?

Note: Read John 12:4-6. Judas had a very different set of values. He didn't accept Christ as his Teacher and Lord. He apparently preferred to surrender to the prince of this world.

7. What command did Jesus give His disciples in John 13:34-35? Why did He say it was new? Why will the person who obeys this command be recognized by all as Christ's disciple? (See John 15:12-17).

Note: In what sense was this commandment new? Until this time, the Jewish rule was to love your neighbor as yourself (Leviticus 19:18). Now, under the new covenant, we are to love one another *as Jesus loved us.* (See 1 John 3:16.)

8. Do you think Peter was sincere when he made the verbal commitment that he would give his life for Christ? If he was sincere, then why did he fail? (See Romans 7:18-25 and John 15:5).

STUDY #15—JOHN 14

A. John 14:1-12

1. In previous chapters we saw that the disciples were beginning to understand that believing in Christ led to a life of clashes with the world's value system. The question arises, How then shall we live in this world? Is there a place for us? Where is it? (John 14:2-3). (See also 1 Corinthians 12:21-31.) The answer is a new union with Christ, with the Father, and with other disciples, who are the body of Christ.

2. Jesus tells His disciples they have already seen God the Father. Philip takes exception to this, asking Christ to show them the Father. Jesus responds by reaffirming that they indeed have already seen the Father. In what sense was this true? (See John 5:19,30; 8:28; 12:49,50; 14:11).

   Note: What was the origin of what Christ said? What was the origin of Christ's works? Whose will did Christ obey?

   Conclusion: In seeing Christ, they saw the Father.

B. John 14:12-20

3. What did Christ say would happen to anyone who believed in Him? (14:12).

4. On what basis could Jesus make such a bold claim to a group of common men who would soon be left on their own? (14:16-20).

5. Who is this other "Counselor"? (14:16).

   Note: Jesus told the disciples that He would send someone to them. (See John 14:16-17.) Then He told them that He Himself would return (14:18-20). Later He insisted that not only He, but also His Father, would inhabit them (14:23). How do you understand this apparent paradox?

6. What was the relationship between Christ and the Father? (See 14:10).

What is the relationship between Christ and those who believe in Him? (See John 14:10, 15:5).

We now have our definition of a Christian. What is it? (See Romans 8:9).

What resource did Christ offer in order that great things could take place in our lives? (14:12-14).

C. John 14:21-31

7. What promise is made to those who, out of love, obey Christ? Why is obedience a necessary requirement to a more intimate understanding of Christ?

In John 14:15,21,23 we find three necessary elements to our growth in Christ. What are they, and in what sequence must they occur? What are Christ's commandments? (See 1 John 3:23).

8. What does the Holy Spirit do for the Christian? (14:26). How does He teach us? (See 2 Timothy 3:16).

9. What is the difference between Christ's peace and the peace of the world? (See 2 Thessalonians 3:16 and Philippians 4:6-7).

STUDY #16—JOHN 15

In the first part of this chapter, we see that Jesus compared the relationship between Himself and the Christian to that of the vine and its branches in order to communicate a central truth in the Christian life.

A. John 15:1-8

1. Vines produce grapes. If Christ is the vine and the Christian is the branch, what fruit does the Christian produce?

   Note: Christ produces after His kind. His personality is reproduced in the Christian. This is a supernatural phenomenon. This is why He said, "Apart from me you can do nothing." (15:5). (See also Galatians 5:22-23 and 1 Corinthians 13:1-8.)

   What are the implications of Jesus' claim that He is the true vine? (See Luke 6:43-45). He is the only kind of vine that produces true life.

2. Answer the following questions on spiritual fruit-bearing.
   a. According to verse 8, what is the purpose of the branch that bears fruit?

      Note: The purpose is to glorify the Father. (See 1 Corinthians 10:31.)
   b. What does it mean to glorify the Father?

      Note: Read John 14:7 and 17:4. Christ's function while on earth was to glorify His Father—that is, to show who and what the Father is. A true disciple will serve the same function.
   c. What happens to the branch that does not produce fruit? (15:2).

      Note: Violent removal takes place. (See 1 Corinthians 5:5-7, 11:29-32.) All dead wood must be removed. Every living branch must be drastically cut back to prevent the excessive growth of leaves and limbs so that more fruit can grow. Although this seems to be a painful process, those who have suffered most are usually the most fruitful.

d. What happens to branches that do produce fruit?
Note: They, too, are pruned. (See 2 Timothy 3:16-17, James 1:2-3, and Hebrews 12:4-13.)

3. What is the secret of producing fruit?
Note: Dependence or abiding is the key. What does it mean to abide? (See John 5:19-30, 8:28-31, and Romans 12:1-2).

Note: As Jesus was dependent on the Father in everything, so must the Christian be dependent on Christ. How can this be done? (See John 5:19,30; 8:28-31; and Romans 12:1-2).

What happens to those who live independently of Christ? (15:6).

Why does Christ offer a blank check to any person who abides in Him? (15:7). (See also 1 John 5:14-15 and James 4:2-4.) His Word remains in those who abide in Him to teach them what to ask for.

B. John 15:9-27

4. According to John 15:9-27, what can the person who is dependent on Christ expect in return?
Note:
a. Because we are recipients of Christ's love, we know Him better. What does His love consist of? He sacrificed Himself (15:13); He sought intimacy (15:15); and He took the initiative (15:16).
b. Peace.
c. Joy.
d. Loving others as He loves them, becoming their true friends, and thereby assisting them to become His disciples as well (15:12-17).
e. A new relationship with the world: conflict (15:18-20). Why does the world hate Christ and His

disciples? Because they are different (15:19); because they don't know God (15:21); and because He reveals their sin (15:22-25). What are two ways of changing this particular attitude of the world? (15:26-27). Answer: The work of the Holy Spirit and the testimony of the disciples' changed lives.

STUDY #17—JOHN 16:1-15

This is the last of four consecutive chapters in which Christ gave His disciples some final instructions. Without doubt, He took advantage of His last few hours with them to underline those things that were of the greatest importance in their lives.

By way of review:

    a. What attitudes did Jesus teach His disciples? (chapter 13).

    b. What provision did He promise them in the light of His imminent departure? (chapter 14).

    c. What is the key word in chapter 15? What does it mean?

A. John 16:1-7

1. In the previous chapter we saw how Jesus showed the inevitability of the world's hatred. In chapter 16 we see Him clarify the implications of that situation. How did the disciples react to this clarification? (16:6).

2. In John 16 we see Jesus speaking at length of the provisions He was arranging for His disciples for after His departure. Notice in verse 7 that He even claimed that they would be better off after He was gone. How could that be true? (See John 14:16-20 and 1 Corinthians 2:11-16).

Note: The intimacy of all human relationships is limited by physical separation. Jesus said that He had to leave, thereby discarding His physical limitation. But He emphasized that He would return to cohabit our bodies with us. When this happens, we enjoy a greater level of intimacy with Him than even the apostles did while they walked with Him.

B. John 16:8-11

3. What three things does the Holy Spirit communicate to the nonChristian?

Note: In John 16:8-11, the word "because" occurs three times. In each case, it is followed by a dependent clause, intended to explain the primary clause. At first glance these dependent clauses appear to explain nothing. But how should we understand these verses?

a. What does the word "sin" mean in verse 9?

Note: (See Isaiah 53:6, John 3:36, and John 5:40.) In this case, sin refers to a deliberate refusal to believe in Christ.

b. According to 16:10, how is justice obtained?

Note: By Christ's return to the Father. (See Romans 5:18, 8:31-34, 1 Peter 3:18, and John 11:51.)

c. According to 16:11, who is under "judgment"?

Note: Who rules the world? (See John 12:31 and Matthew 4:8-10). The Spirit of God convinces the individual that he is on a shipwrecked planet that has no future. (See 2 Peter 3:7.)

C. John 16:12-15

4. What does Jesus promise that the Holy Spirit will do for the Christian? (16:13-15).

a. He will guide the Christian into all truth.

b. He will glorify Christ.

5. How will the Spirit guide Christians into all truth? (16:13).
    Note: By opening their eyes to God's plan.

6. What does it mean to glorify Christ? (16:14).
    Note: The Spirit shows how Christ fulfills His plan in Christians.

STUDY #18—JOHN 16:16-33

1. Jesus foresaw a crisis in the lives of His disciples.
    a. What was this crisis? (16:16-22).
        Note: While they suffered and cried, the world would rejoice.
    b. What would bring on this crisis?
        Note: His departure.
    c. Why would His departure from them bring about the crisis?
        Note: (See Mark 14:27-42.) The disciples would behave like cowards, their faith would disintegrate, and they would feel the embarrassment of those who had just been victimized by a charlatan.
    d. What good would come out of this crisis? (16:22-23).
        Note: The disciples would become steadfast and mature. While they were in the depths of their despondency, they would realize the reality of Jesus' resurrection. Then, they were to become indomitable. No one could destroy the resulting joy.
    e. Why are crises important for us? (See James 1:1-4, 2 Corinthians 7:8-10, Deuteronomy 8:2-3, and Hebrews 12:4-13).

2. It is in this context that Jesus offers us the ultimate in terms of spiritual resources. What is it? (16:24).

3. Christ referred to His coming death and resurrection in the expression "in a little while" (16:16). What are the primary benefits of His great victory over death for the Christian?

   a. Permanent happiness (16:20,22).

   b. Answered prayers (16:23-27).

   c. Peace and victory over the world system (16:33).

4. Why does God answer prayers made in Jesus' name, even without a mediator? (16:26-27).

   Note: Our love for Christ and our faith in Him give us the rights of children of God.

STUDY #19—JOHN 17

A. John 17:1-5

1. What is your concept of eternal life?

   Note: Generally, we think of it in terms of something that God offers us and that in turn becomes ours. We receive it as a gift. What new insight do we get about eternal life from 17:3?

   Eternal life is not a state of being but a personal relationship with Christ's being. What do you think this means? (See John 14:6 and 1 John 5:11-12).

2. How can we know God? (See John 14:6-10 and 1 John 5:20).

   How do we discover who Jesus is? (17:3).

   a. From the Scriptures. (See John 5:39.)

   b. Through His death, resurrection, and return to the Father. (See John 12:23-33, 13:31-36.)

      First the Father was revealed by the Son; now the Son is being revealed by the Father.

B. John 17:4-26

3. What was the work Jesus accomplished for the Father? (17:4).

Note: He multiplied Himself by eleven. (See Mark 3:14-15 and Luke 6:12-13.)

4. How did Jesus go about accomplishing this multiplication?
   a. He transmitted the Scriptures to His disciples in such a way that they could believe and live in accordance with them (17:6-8).
   b. He was with them (17:9-13).
   c. He prayed for them—that they would be able to withstand the pressures of a world that thought and acted differently than they did (17:9-11).
   d. He took care of them so that they wouldn't lose their way (17:12-17).
   e. He trusted them with His mission (17:18-19).
   f. He prayed that they might come to be the kind of team that He and the Father were (17:20-26).

5. What single means did the Father provide so that the message of redemption would reach the world? (See 2 Corinthians 5:18-21 and 2 Timothy 2:2). The means was the multiplication of workers.

6. In what way do you wish to participate in this mission? What is your part in this process?

STUDY #20—JOHN 18

Jesus realized that He was under the sentence of death (John 11:53). Knowing this, He planned His activities in such a way that the sinfulness of man would have ample opportunity to reveal itself. Jesus began to take certain precautions (11:54), which led the religious authorities to also take certain precautions (11:57).

A. John 18:1-7

1. What steps did the religious authorities have to take in order to arrest and imprison Jesus?

    What, exactly, did Judas's betrayal consist of?

    Note: He was one of the select few who knew the places where Jesus wandered alone.

B. John 18:8-24

2. What measures and arguments had to be employed in order to condemn Jesus before the court?

    Note: (See Mark 14:53-65 and John 19:7.) Violence, fraud, and distortion of His words took place.

3. The religious authorities, examining the case theologically, condemned Him on what ground?

    Note: (See Leviticus 24:15-16, Matthew 26:57-68, and Acts 7:51.) The so-called ground was blasphemy.

C. John 18:25-37

4. In the civil court, what accusations did the Jews use to obtain a conviction?

    Note: Overthrowing the political regime. (See Mark 15:1-15.)

5. What conclusion did the civil authorities arrive at after trying the case? (See John 18:38).

    What was Pilate's attitude during the trial? Why did he permit the execution?

    What motivated Pilate to ask the question stated in John 18:38?

Note: Pilate's attitude was, "As long as I am merely searching for the truth, I am not responsible for anything at all."

6. Why did the Jewish officials want to leave Jesus in the hands of the Romans, in a civil court, rather than trying His case according to the Jewish system? (18:31). These cunning, insecure Jewish officials wanted to make a political criminal of Jesus, thus de-emphasizing His religious role.

7. What was the real reason that the religious authorities demanded Jesus' death? (See Matthew 26:63-66). Accepting Him as God the Son, the Messiah, would have meant accepting Him as king. That would have meant personal submission.

8. The imprisonment and judgment of Jesus underscores the sinfulness of man and the corruption of man's religious and civil systems. What did that time of Jesus' trial reveal about His disciples? (18:8-11, 15-18). (See also Mark 14:50, 66-72.)

   How can these actions on the part of the disciples be explained?

   Note: (See John 13:36-38 and 2 Corinthians 10:3-4.) A person left to himself is virtually incapable of following Christ, even if his intentions seem to be fully sincere. It is only while a person is under the control of the Holy Spirit that he becomes capable of being faithful in his actions.

9. In summary, what quality do all the characters in this chapter's study, other than Jesus Himself, have in common?

   Note: Injustice. (See Romans 3:9-18.)

STUDY #21—JOHN 19

A. John 19:1-16

1. The treatment that Jesus suffered at the hands of the religious and civil authorities was not normal. The two criminals who were crucified with Him did not receive the same treatment.

   Note:

   a. The religious authorities who condemned Jesus for the crime of blasphemy did not execute Him in accordance with their own laws (19:6-7). (See also Leviticus 24:15-16 and Deuteronomy 21:21-23.)

   b. The ridicule by the soldiers was excessive (19:2-5). If He was a political criminal, why then was He mocked? This was irrational hatred and scorn. (See Psalm 69:4 and Luke 18:31-34.)

   c. The religious authorities sacrificed their own convictions in order to obtain His execution (19:15).

   Note: In John 8:33-47 we saw that they did not admit that they were under the domain of the Roman Empire. Now, all of a sudden, they were loyal Roman subjects!

B. John 19:17-30

2. When Jesus perceived that He had fulfilled His mission, He said, "I thirst." What kind of thirst was this? (See Mark 15:33-37 and Luke 16:24-28). It was the thirst that comes from being separated from God. It seems paradoxical that He who offered living water died thirsty. (See Galatians 3:13.)

3. What was "completed"? (19:28). (See also John 12:24-27 and Mark 10:45.)

4. Why did God allow all this to take place? (See Isaiah 53:10-12).

5. Why was God so strict in demanding that Christ go through all this? (See Romans 6:23). Because of the integrity of God's justice.

6. What led God to act this way toward His Son?
   Note: (See John 3:16, 1 John 4:10, and Isaiah 53:4-12.) Note God's dilemma: to be just and loving at the same time. Read Romans 5:6-21.

7. The blood of Christ, shed on the Cross, has an important meaning to Christianity. What is it? (See 1 Corinthians 6:19, 1 Peter 1:18-19, 1 John 1:7, Romans 3:19-26, Revelation 1:5, and Hebrews 9:11-24). It is the price God paid for our ransom. This certainly seems illogical to philosophers and unnecessary to the religious legalists, but it is the only true basis for the Christian's salvation. (See 1 Corinthians 1:18-25.)

C. John 19:31-42

8. What prompted Joseph of Arimathea and Nicodemus, who had concealed the fact they were disciples because they were fearful of getting caught, to now make such a bold move at such a precarious time as this? (See 2 Corinthians 5:14-15).
   Christ's death forced them to take a stand. With Christ it is all the way or not at all.

9. Death on a cross was usually caused by asphyxia (lack of air in the lungs). Thus, in order to make the death faster, the Roman soldiers used to break the victims' legs. No longer able to raise themselves by pushing up with their

legs against the cross thus enabling them to breathe, they soon suffocated. Why didn't the Roman soldiers break Jesus' legs? (19:31-37).

What really caused Christ's death (other than the crucifixion itself)?

> a. Carrying the burden of our sins. (See 2 Corinthians 5:21, Romans 5:21, and Romans 6:23.)
> b. His own decision. (See John 10:18 and Luke 23:46.)

STUDY #22—JOHN 20

A. John 20:1-18

1. What were the reactions of the disciples when they discovered that the tomb was empty?
   a. They were convinced that they had been deceived and that the body had been stolen (20:2). (See also Matthew 28:11-15.)
   b. Fear (20:5).
   c. Lack of understanding of what the Scriptures had predicted (20:9). (See also Luke 24:25-27.)
   d. The kind of unhappiness caused by unbelief (20:11-15).
   e. Spiritual blindness (20:14-15). (See also Luke 24:13-35.)

   Man is blind to what is inconceivable from his point of view. Resurrection was something that had never happened before in all human history.

2. What evidence did the disciples have for Christ's resurrection?
   a. The stone was removed (20:1). The tomb carved out of rock was sealed with a circular stone weighing several tons. Such a stone could be easily set into position by rolling it down a ramp, but several people were needed

to remove it. Notice that the door was not opened to let Christ out but to let the disciples in to see that He was gone.
   b. The empty tomb. The burial cloth had been laid aside (20:3-8).
   c. The presence of angels (20:12-13).
   d. The prophecy of Christ Himself and of the prophets. (See Luke 24:25-27.)

      None of this, however, persuaded the disciples to believe. What did it take?

      Note: It took a personal encounter with the resurrected Lord (20:14-16). (See also Mark 16:1-16.) Things are no different today. It takes more than mere apologetics to produce faith. One must still meet the person of Christ. (See 1 Corinthians 2:4-7.)

3. What was different about Jesus after He had risen from the dead?
   a. On some occasions the disciples did not recognize Jesus (20:14). (See also Luke 24:15-16.) He wasn't always recognizable to the human way of seeing.
   b. He wasn't limited by our physical laws (20:19-20). (See also Luke 24:31,36-43 and 1 Corinthians 15:35-49.) He had a new body that didn't have the ordinary human limitations.

4. What new relationship did Jesus' resurrection allow between Him and His disciples? (20:17). (See also 1 John 3:1-3 and 1 Corinthians 15:50-58.)

B. John 20:24-31
5. Normally, what happens when someone arrives at the conviction that Jesus is the Christ? (20:29-31).

      In what way was Thomas (the proverbial "doubting

Thomas") an exception to this rule? (20:24-29). (See also Matthew 12:38-40, Luke 16:31, and John 4:48.)

Note: In all these passages we see Jesus stating that miracles do not produce faith. A person who asks for signs has a moral hang-up, not intellectual doubts, in his relationship with God.

6. What is the meaning of Thomas's statement when he recognized the resurrected Christ? (20:28).

He stated that he personally accepted Christ as his Lord and God.

7. When He was with the disciples after His resurrection, Christ gave them a mission and the capacity to accomplish it. What was it, and how does this mission affect your life? (20:19-23). (See also Matthew 28:18-20, Mark 16:15, Luke 24:45-47, and Acts 1:8.)

STUDY #23—JOHN 21

A. John 21:1-14

1. Peter is perhaps the dominant character in chapter 21, as much by his actions as by his part in the conversations. What characteristic qualities of Peter are evident here?
   a. Individualism (21:2-3).
   b. Impulsiveness (21:7).
   c. Self-sufficiency.

   When Jesus met Simon, He nicknamed him Cephas, which means "Rock" (John 1:42). What did He mean by that?

2. The following two passages show some of Peter's biggest blunders: Matthew 16:13-23 and Matthew 17:2-6. He still

hadn't quite understood who Christ really was. He had the "honor" of having his attention drawn to this fact by God Himself.

3. What had to happen to Peter to teach him to listen to Christ? (See Mark 14:17-31, 66-72). Why did he come to the point of behaving in an even more deplorable manner than the others?

B. John 21:15-23
4. What did Christ want to verify with this series of three questions? (21:15-17).

Note: Whether or not Peter was cured of his excessive self-confidence.

What is the only true motive for serving Christ? (21:15-17). Loving Him!

5. After Christ verified that Peter was in a position to listen and trust Him, what responsibility did He give to Peter? (21:15-17).

6. And did Peter learn? (See 1 Peter 5:1-14 and 2 Peter 1:12-15).

7. One of the first things Jesus said to Peter was "Follow me" (Mark 1:16-18). Peter liked the idea, and so he followed. Now, at the end, Christ renewed this same invitation! Why was the second invitation more significant than the first? (21:18-22).

Note: Peter was now better equipped to understand and serve.

8. What would feeding and taking care of the sheep eventually cost Peter? (21:18-19). (See also John 10:11-15.)

Final Question: What permanent results have taken place in your life as a result of studying the Gospel of John?

STUDY #24: THE 24TH HOUR WITH JOHN
(The Bridge Illustration Based on John's Gospel)

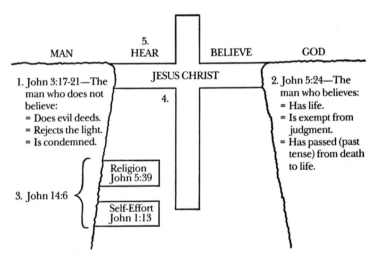

1. Man is separated from God and is under judgment because of sin (John 3:17-21, 36). (See also Romans 3:23, 6:23, and Hebrews 9:27.)

2. The many statements made by Jesus about eternal life indicate there is a solution to this separation (John 5:24).

3. Man attempts to build his own bridges (John 1:13), but Jesus declares Himself to be the Way (John 14:6). (See also Ephesians 2:8-9.)

4. Jesus is the Way because of who He is: God (John 1:14); the Lamb (John 1:35) . . . and because of what He did: He died (John 6:51; See also Romans 5:8); He rose from the dead (John 11:25).

5. Jesus calls on us to act on this message—to hear and believe (John 5:24). Synonyms: Receive (John 1:12); be reborn (John 3:3); drink (John 4:13; See also Revelation 3:20).

*The DISCIPLESHIP TODAY Series
is designed to call lay men and
women to a Christ-centered,
practical discipleship in our
contemporary world. The challenge
of following Jesus Christ through the
disorienting cultural changes,
pressures to conform, and
opportunities for witness and service
presented by modern life requires a
God-given discernment. Spiritual
men and women want to respond to
the needs of their world with actions
that are timely and relevant—yet
are motivated and measured by
God's Word and directed by His
Holy Spirit. The books in this series
are intended to help today's disciples
respond to the concerns of our day
with a sensitivity born of the mind
of Christ and an agenda for action
set by the purposes of God.*